CHAUCER

CANTERBURY TALES

NOTES

COLES EDITORIAL BOARD

Bound to stay open

Publisher's Note
Otabind (Ota-bind). This book has been bound using the patented Otabind process. You can open this book at any page, gently run your finger down the spine, and the pages will lie flat.

ABOUT COLES NOTES

COLES NOTES have been an indispensible aid to students on five continents since 1948.

COLES NOTES are available for a wide range of individual literary works. Clear, concise explanations and insights are provided along with interesting interpretations and evaluations.

Proper use of COLES NOTES will allow the student to pay greater attention to lectures and spend less time taking notes. This will result in a broader understanding of the work being studied and will free the student for increased participation in discussions.

COLES NOTES are an invaluable aid for review and exam preparation as well as an invitation to explore different interpretive paths.

COLES NOTES are written by experts in their fields. It should be noted that any literary judgement expressed herein is just that — the judgement of one school of thought. Interpretations that diverge from, or totally disagree with any criticism may be equally valid.

COLES NOTES are designed to supplement the text and are not intended as a substitute for reading the text itself. Use of the NOTES will serve not only to clarify the work being studied, but should enhance the reader's enjoyment of the topic.

ISBN 0-7740-3410-6

© COPYRIGHT 1996 AND PUBLISHED BY
COLES PUBLISHING COMPANY
TORONTO—CANADA
PRINTED IN CANADA

Manufactured by Webcom Limited
Cover finish: Webcom's Exclusive **Duracoat**

CONTENTS

Geoffrey Chaucer: Life and Works

Geoffrey Chaucer, one of the greatest of English writers, made his living as a civil servant and composed poetry as a hobby. His career, however, contributed to his literary growth.

He was born about 1343 of a prosperous family and reared in London. His father, a wine importer, was able to find him a position (in 1357 or earlier) as a page-boy in the household of King Edward III's daughter-in-law, Elizabeth of Ulster. From this period on, despite the political uncertainties of the age, Chaucer enjoyed the uninterrupted favor of the members of the court of, successively, Edward, Richard II and Henry IV, both as a man of affairs and as a poet.

Chaucer served as a soldier in France in the campaigns of the Hundred Years War in 1359-1360 and was sent abroad on at least seven occasions between 1368 and 1387, either to France or Italy, on diplomatic missions. He acquired the training necessary for business, probably at the law school known as the Inner Temple. He acted in London as a Controller of Customs from 1374 to 1385, became a Justice of the Peace in Kent in 1385 and a member of Parliament for the county in 1386, served in London again from 1389 to 1391 as a Clerk of the Works, and was thereafter awarded a less active royal appointment.

He was married (c.1366) to Philippa de Roet of Flanders, who was lady-in-waiting to the queen and sister-in-law to John of Gaunt. Records suggest that he had two sons and a daughter and that his wife died in 1387. Chaucer died in 1400 in a house he had rented in the grounds of Westminster Abbey. He was buried in that section of the Abbey later to become famous as the Poets' Corner.

Major Works
The Book of the Duchess
The Canterbury Tales
The House of Fame
The Legend of Good Women
The Parliament of Fowls
Troilus and Criseyde

Minor Works
A Ballad of Complaint

A Complaint to His Lady
Against Unconstant Women
An A.B.C.
Anelida and Arcite
A Treatise on the Astrolabe
Chaucer's Envoy to Bukton
Chaucer's Envoy to Scogan
Chaucer's Words to Adam, His Own Scribe
The Complaint of Chaucer to His Purse
The Complaint of Mars
The Complaint of Venus
The Complaint Unto Pity
The Former Age
Fortune
Gentility
Lack of Steadfastness
Merciles Beaute
To Rosamond
Truth
Womanly Nobleness

Translations
Consolation of Philosophy (Boethius)
The Romance of the Rose (Jean de Meun & Guillaume
     de Lorris)

Chaucer's Development as a Poet

The growth of Chaucer's genius can be illustrated by four works. In *The Book of the Duchess* the poet dreams that he shares the grief of a lonely young knight, who proves to be John of Gaunt mourning his newly lost first wife. The conception is original and the expression of sympathy is gracefully tender, but the framework of the dream-vision and the knight's description of his love are strongly influenced by French models.

In the uncompleted *House of Fame*, another dream-vision, the poet is carried off by an eagle to learn whether those who are in the service of Love are happy or not. The self-confident and domineering eagle was suggested to Chaucer by his reading of Dante's *Paradiso*, but here it plays a comic role in a work that tends to parody the artificiality of medieval courtly love conventions.

Troilus and Criseyde, in which he amplified Boccaccio's pseudo-classical romance, *Il Filostrato*, was Chaucer's first major achievement. In *The Canterbury Tales*, a masterpiece even greater than *Troilus* (though uncompleted), Chaucer turned to the English scene and excelled all the writers of his era in his delineation of the men, women, children and animals familiar to him in real life. A richly assorted group of pilgrims entertain themselves by telling stories on the way from London to Canterbury. Through his descriptions in the "General Prologue" and dramatizations in the links connecting the tales he portrays in detail seven members of the feudal order, thirteen people associated with religious life and fourteen townspeople — the chivalrous Knight, the aristocratic Prioress, the fraudulent Pardoner, the impoverished Canon's Yeoman, the amorous Wife of Bath, the reticent civil servant who is Chaucer himself, and the rest who have gained an independent identity as real as that of Falstaff, Tom Jones or Becky Sharp. And the tales Chaucer has supplied match the tellers in their rich variety — the Knight's courtly romance, the Miller's racy fabliau, the Second Nun's pious saint's life, the Nun's Priest's mock-heroic fable, the Pardoner's hypocritical sermon and the Parson's sincere one.

Like most medieval craftsmen, Chaucer, whether as young apprentice or as mature master, followed the pattern of established models. His success can therefore be partially explained by his reading of "old, approved stories." Sources or analogues have been found for almost all of his works and even for his style. His comic tone, for instance, often seems reminiscent of his favorite Latin poet, Ovid, and his philosophical ideas are usually those of Boethius. He appears to have borrowed materials in turn from the French — from Machaut, Deschamps, Froissart — then from the Italians — from Dante, Petrarch and Boccaccio — and finally, perhaps, from his fellow countryman Langland. But the ultimate achievements of the medieval master craftsman were profoundly original. Chaucer's skill as a teller of tales; his deftness of characterization and description; his perfection in metrical technique; his understanding of man's religious, moral and philosophical instincts; his knowledge of life and acceptance of its mingled tragedy and comedy and his transcendent sense of humor are, in combination, unique.

Chaucer's World

The technological differences between our age and Chaucer's are obvious enough when we think of the weird astrological-medical theories of the Physician (Prologue 411-44), or of the fact that it took Chaucer's pilgrims three days of hard travel to traverse the sixty miles between London and Canterbury. The differences in society and its assumptions are important in understanding the actions and attitudes of Chaucer's pilgrims.

The social structure of England (and all Europe) in the 14th century was feudal. Power radiated from the king, through his nobles (when he could control them), and through their subjects, with little kingly power reaching the lower echelons of society. The king and his nobles owned the land, which was divided into large agricultural estates. These provided the men, material and money to support the crown and its wars. Society was organized in a hierarchical form, one's wealth and power being a matter of what position one occupied on the hierarchical ladder. This ladder extended from the king, through the great noblemen-landlords (like Chaucer's patron, John of Gaunt, Duke of Lancaster), down through lesser landlords and their various executive officers with, at the bottom, the serfs who worked the land for their masters. It is important to note that while we regard this system as unjust and oppressive, the medieval people could conceive of no other. Each level of society had its rights and privileges, and each had its duties and obligations. Despite the occasional abuse, they regarded the system as right and proper.

Three groups of Chaucer's pilgrims may be isolated to suggest how this system worked. The first represents agricultural feudalism (the first and basic kind) founded on land ownership and service. The Knight, who is the highest on the scale, is a landowner, and has therefore served in the wars for his king. He will be followed in this by his son, the Squire. The Knight's Yeoman is a servant, whose only duty is to the Knight. The Franklin also holds land, perhaps "in fee" from some noble, but more probably in his own right. His service is the direction of his farm, his obligation to the noble or king being doubtless in the form of the yearly harvest and of men in time of need. The Miller does not himself own land but has been given the right to mill all grain on an estate. The Reeve manages an estate. They are both servants, but of an exalted kind, and make shrewd and profitable use of their power, as we shall see. The lowest in the hierarchy is the Plowman, who simply tills the land.

England was changing in the 14th century, and one of the most important changes was the growth of a new, urban society (mainly in London) where the feudal structure was somewhat modified. Neither the Physician nor the Man of Law owned land, although they were both men of substance. The Physician (Chaucer tells us) made money out of the Plague, and the Lawyer made money out of almost everything. They were the beginning of a new class, today called professional people. The Manciple and the Merchant and even the Wife of Bath (who is a clothmaker) also represent the urbanization process. They were not directly commanded by anyone, and in time they became the mercantile middle class who overthrew the monarchy and the last vestiges of feudalism in the civil war of the 17th century. It is also significant that the Haberdasher, the Carpenter, the Weaver, the Dyer and the Carpet Maker are presented together, in that they are all members of one of the great parish guilds. It was through these craft and parish guild associations that the new urban artisans achieved the power that they lacked through not belonging to the land-hierarchy.

There is yet a third group, constituting a kind of feudal system of its own, and representing one of the most powerful elements of medieval society — the church. Nine of Chaucer's thirty pilgrims belong to the clergy, and it would be difficult to overestimate the importance of the Roman Catholic church to the lives of the people of western Europe in the 14th century. They might disregard its teaching (as some of the pilgrims do) or complain of its abuses (as Chaucer does), but from baptism, through confirmation and marriage, to the funeral rites, it was intimately connected with their lives. It was a visible force throughout England, from the great cathedrals — such as Canterbury — and the religious houses, down to the humble parish churches.

Despite the worldly aspects of life that often appear in *The Canterbury Tales*, we should not forget that the people Chaucer gathers together are pilgrims and that the occasion for their gathering is the spring pilgrimage to the shrine of "the holy blisfil martir," St. Thomas à Becket, at Canterbury. We can gauge the importance of the church in people's lives by noting how many varieties of belief or simulated belief Chaucer presents. They run all the way from the dedicated holiness of the Parson, through the superficial observances of the Prioress, to the outright hypocrisy of the Summoner and Pardoner. Chaucer, looking about him, sees fit to define a large proportion of his characters by where they stand with regard to the church.

It is sometimes suggested that medieval times were happier, simpler and less troubled than our own. In some ways this is true — certainly Chaucer's pilgrims are free from many of our modern anxieties — yet the 14th century had its own troubles, and it is an oversimplification to regard it as a time of innocent good humor. In fact, it is the overall good humor of Chaucer's treatment that has fostered this view, and while he is basically optimistic, he would be unlikely to accept it.

The Plague, or Black Death (to which Chaucer occasionally alludes), entered England in mid-century with dreadful consequences. It is said that half the population was wiped out. While this may be an exaggeration, it is no exaggeration to say that people lived in constant fear of the ravages of the Plague. Two of its effects were inflated prices and a further depression of the already grim living conditions of those at the bottom of the economic ladder. This in turn produced the insurrection known as the Peasants' Revolt (1381), in which the infuriated mob murdered many of those whom they regarded as their exploiters. Chaucer — as a Justice of the Peace and a Member of Parliament — might be expected to be bitter about this unprecedented attack on the social order. It may be a measure of his generosity that only a few years after the rebellion his portrait of the Plowman in the "Prologue" is remarkable for its praise of the peasant virtues.

The Hundred Years War continued, with the French threatening to invade England. This is one of the reasons for the warlike nature of Chaucer's Shipman, whose merchant ship was obliged to be a fighting vessel. It also accounts for the Merchant's anxiety about trade if the shipping route between Middelburg in the Netherlands and Orwell in England is broken.

The church itself was divided at the time, one faction having a pope at Rome and the other at Avignon, with some of

Europe (including England) supporting the first and some (including Scotland) the second. The confusion resulting from this situation was probably in part the cause of the clerical abuses that produced so much complaint (some of it in *The Canterbury Tales*) during the period.

If we set these disruptions alongside the achievements of art and literature, the security of a stable society, and the calm that comes from faith (the qualities usually presented as typical of the Middle Ages), we shall probably be somewhere near the truth. At any rate, it was a time of transition and great variety: an appropriate time for the creation of a work as varied and multicolored as *The Canterbury Tales*.

Chaucer's Language

The language that Chaucer wrote and spoke was different from modern English. The scholars of our day call the language of Chaucer's age, in retrospect, Middle English, thereby differentiating it both from its ancestor, Old English or Anglo-Saxon, spoken before 1066, and from its descendant, our modern English, spoken after 1500. But Chaucer, we must remember, would have considered his language normal, modern English. His particular dialect, among the diverse regional and class dialects of England, was that spoken by the educated classes of London during the 14th century. It later became the model for standard English when other dialects began to lose prestige.

Unfortunately for the subsequent appreciation of Chaucer's work, however, language is ever-changing. Consciously or unconsciously, speakers make minor changes within the limited sets of distinctive sounds, intonations, grammatical forms, sentence patterns and words currently in use. In time the subtle balance within these sets of interdependent speech elements is changed so that the language of yesterday seems unnatural or obscure. The changes in the English language, particularly in its pattern of contrasting sounds, were remarkably extensive in the century after Chaucer's death in 1400. Presumably, if Chaucer had reappeared in the age of Shakespeare, two centuries later, Elizabethans would have found his speech almost incomprehensible, not merely because he used words that had become archaic but particularly because an extensive shift of vowel sounds had rendered the still surviving words and grammatical forms that he used unrecognizable in sound. By contrast, three and a half centuries after the death of Shakespeare, we ourselves should find the English spoken in the Elizabethan age still understandable.

By a process of ingenious deductions from the written records of Chaucer's language, scholars have established the principal features of sound, intonation, form, arrangement and vocabulary characteristic of the language actually spoken in his time. The following simplified account of these findings offers a practical working guide for those who wish to understand what Chaucer wrote and to read his poetry aloud in the manner in which the poet would have read it.

Pronunciation

To transform the written transcript of Chaucer's language consistently into spoken words, the first requirement is a readjustment of our sense of relationship between spelling symbols and spoken sounds.

(1) Pronounce all consonants as we do those in modern English. However, *gh*, as in *night*, though now silent, was pronounced like the *ch* in the Scottish pronunciation of *loch* or in the German pronounciation of *Bach*.

(2) Pronounce all the syllables in a word, even those represented only by a final *e* which is no longer pronounced in modern English. Thus, pronounce Chaucer's *dame* with two syllables as *dahmeh*, and his *dames* as *dahmess*. It is most important for our understanding of Chaucer's metres to note that, as in classical French poetry, all final syllables were pronounced.

(3) Pronounce all vowels according to their so-called "Continental" values, that is, according to the sounds that they represent in modern French or Italian, or in our modern pronunciation of Latin. Thus, pronounce the vowel *a*, as in Chaucer's *dame*, as the *ah* sound of modern French *dame* (or modern English *father*), not as the *ay* sound of modern English *dame*. Other instances are Chaucer's *bare, care, fame, game, hate, lame, make, page, rage, save, take, wake.*

Pronounce the vowel *e* or *ee*, as in Chaucer's *regioun*, as the *ay* sound of modern French *région* (or modern English *able*) not as the *ee* sound of modern English *region*. Other instances are Chaucer's *be, me, thee*. There are a large number of exceptions in this case, but the important fact to remember is that Chaucer's *e* is never pronounced as the *ee* sound of modern English *region, be*, and so on.

Pronounce the vowel *i* or *y*, as in Chaucer's *fine*, as the *ee* sound in modern French *fine* (or modern English *machine*) not as the *eye* sound in modern English *fine*. Other instances are *bite, glide, kynde* (modern English *kind*), *mine, prime, ride, strive, thine, wyn* (modern English *wine*).

Pronounce the vowels *ou* or *ow*, as in Chaucer's *doute*, as the *ou* sound in modern French *doute* (or modern English *soup*) not as the *ow* sound in modern English *doubt*. Instances are *bour* (modern English *bower*), *doute* (modern English *doubt*), *foul, hous, mous, tour* (modern English *tower*), *out.*

The vowels represented by *o, u,* and diphthongs diverge less notably from modern usage and need not be described here.

Grammar

The grammatical forms used by Chaucer are less troublesome for the modern reader than the now-vanished pronunciation, for contrasting forms can be positively identified from the written record, and most of them survive, at least as archaisms, in modern English.

Nouns

The numerous declensional systems derived from the earliest stages of the English language had by the time of Chaucer become reduced, with few exceptions, to two contrasting forms:

dissh (dish)	*disshes (dishes)*
disshes (dish's)	*disshes (dishes')*

It must be noticed that the ending *es* was pronounced with an *s*, not, as in modern English *dishes (dishez)*, with a *z*. Nor was the termination conditioned, as in modern English, by the phonetic nature of the noun's final sound. Compare Chaucer's *disshes, cattes*, and *dogges* with the modern three-type system: *dishes (ez), cats (s)* and *dogs (z)*.

Pronouns

There are several important differences between Chaucer's pronouns and those used in modern English, as the following chart will show.

I		*thou*	*we*		*ye*
myn		*thyn*	*our*		*your*
me		*thee*	*us*		*you*
he	*(h)it*		*she*		*they*
his	*his*		*her(e), hir(e)*		*her(e), hir(e)*
him	*him* (dat.)		*her(e), hir(e)*		*hem*
	(h)it (acc.)				

The only serious difficulty offered by the above set of pronouns lies in the fact that *her(e)* or *hir(e)* may mean, depending on context either *her* or *their*; and *his* may, as in Shakespeare, mean either *his* or *its*.

Adjectives

Chaucer still observed a distinction, now lost, between two different inflections of the adjective, the so-called strong and weak inflections, which were inherited from earlier English. The strong inflection of adjectives consists of a contrast between an absence of ending in the singular *(yong)* and the presence of a final *e* in the plural *(yonge)*. It occurs after the indefinite article (*a* or *an*), or before an otherwise unmodified plural noun, or after a preposition, or as a predicate:

a *yong* knight	*yonge* knightes
of *yong* folk	of *yonge* knightes
he is *yong*	they been (are) *yonge*

The weak inflection, which has a final *e* in both the singular and the plural *(yonge)*, occurs in all other situations:

the (this, myn) *yonge* knight	the (these, myne) *yonge* knightes
O *yonge* knight	O *yonge* knightes

With adjectives, such as *swete*, which have inherited a final *e* as part of their uninflected form, however, no such distinction can be made because their final *e* appears in all situations:

a *swete* knight	*swete* knightes
the *swete* knight	the *swete* knightes

Verbs

In Chaucer's English the past tense of verbs was formed in two basically different patterns, which still survive. Weak verbs (*love*) added a *d* or *t* to the stem; strong verbs (*drinke*) changed their stem vowel. The conjugational endings of the two classes differed, as they no longer do, only in the indicative singular of the past tense. The final *n* of the conjugational endings and the prefix of the past participle (here inserted in parenthesis) were beginning to disappear from the language. Chaucer used them or not at will.

Present Indicative

I *love*	*drinke*	we *love(n)*	*drinke(n)*
thou *lovest*	*drinkest*	ye *love(n)*	*drinke(n)*
he *loveth*	*drinketh*	they *love(n)*	*drinke(n)*

Subjunctive

I, thou, he *love   drinke*   we, ye, they *love(n)   drinke(n)*

Past Indicative

I	*lovede*	*drank*	we *lovede(n)*	*dronke(n)*
thou	*lovedest*	*dronke*	ye *lovede(n)*	*dronke(n)*
he	*lovede*	*drank*	they *lovede(n)*	*dronke(n)*

Subjunctive

I, thou, he *lovede   dronke*   we, ye, they *lovede(n)   dronke(n)*

Imperative

love   drink(e) (thou)   *loveth   drinketh* (ye)

Past Participle   **Infinitive**

I have *(y)loved   (y)dronke(n)*   to *love(n)   drinke(n)*

Some verbs with stem ending in *d* or *t* regularly contracted the conjugational ending *eth*, as in the following common examples: he *bit* (biddeth), *fint* (findeth), *holt* (holdeth), *list* (listeth), *rit* (rideth), *stant* (standeth).

The only other irregularities of frequent occurrence likely to seem unfamiliar to the modern reader are the verb *to be*, which has the forms *we, ye, they be* or *been* in addition to the familiar *are(n)*; and the following group of verbs that are peculiar both in form and meaning:

I *can*, thou *canst*, he *can*; we, ye, they   (I can, know how)
   conne(n), I *coude*, we *coude(n)*
   (conjugated like *lovede*)

I *may*, thou *mayst*, he *may;* we *mowe(n)*   (I can, am able)
   I *mighte*

I *moot*, thou *moost*, he *moot*;   (I may, must)
   we *moote(n)*, I *moste*

I *woot*, thou *woost*, he *woot*; we *wite(n)*   (I know)
   I *wiste*

Syntax

Modern readers will find little in Chaucer's syntax that seems unfamiliar. Chaucer, like other poets before and since, in composing verse takes the liberty of inverting the word order normal to a prose sentence, but one of the chief characteristics of his style is its clarity. And when, on rare occasions, the logic of his sentence is irregular, it merely matches the unconscious illogicalities of everyday speech.

Vocabulary

Most of Chaucer's words, especially those of frequent occurrence, have survived into modern English and have not notably changed in meaning. Some of his words have, however, become archaic, and their meanings must now be learned just as if they were words in a foreign language. And some apparently familiar words have subtly shifted in meaning since Chaucer's day and must therefore be reinterpreted.

Chaucer himself was well aware of the relativity of language and of culture. "You know . . . that in form of speech there is change within a thousand years," he remarks in *Troilus and Criseyde*, "and that words that then had value now seem remarkably quaint and strange to us." "And yet," the people of the past "spoke them so and," he adds shrewdly, "succeeded as well . . . as men do now."

Ironically but inevitably, Chaucer's writing had suffered misunderstanding and neglect from posterity because of the apparent quaintness and strangeness of its language. In the 17th century, for instance, the brilliant poet and critic John Dryden, even though he admired and imitated Chaucer, failed to recognize Chaucer's metrical skill merely because he did not realize that his final *e*'s were to be pronounced. And, despite all the technical assistance afforded by modern scholarship, the reader of today must still make some adjustment of mind if he is to enjoy the feeling that, when he reads Chaucer's poetry, he is reading the language once spoken by living men and women with minds and hearts like our own.

Versification

Chaucer's repertoire of meters, hitherto unparalleled in English poetry, must have been inspired by his French and Italian contemporaries, whose techniques he probably learned not merely by close observation of their writings but also by personal conversations.

In meter, rhyme and verse-form he shows a consistent skill that appears particularly striking when compared with that of his English contemporaries. In England two entirely different types of versification were currently popular. The one representing a native tradition dating from before the Norman Conquest (1066) was based not upon rhyme or a fixed pattern of stressed syllables but upon alliteration. Surviving examples of its application, contemporary with Chaucer, include such poems as the anonymous romance *Sir Gawain and the Green Knight* and the widely read *Piers Plowman*. But the other type, which Chaucer adopted, was the familiar combination of rhyme and fixed stress-patterns, which had gradually been adopted from the French after the Conquest and had become the dominant type of English versification.

The verse-form most commonly used in England during Chaucer's youth in narrative poetry was the four-beat couplet, and it was in this measure that Chaucer cast some of his earlier poetry, such as the *House of Fame*. But there is a danger that short lines with rhyme recurring every eight syllables will lapse into a tedious jog-trot, as indeed they did in the hands of lesser poets of the 14th century, and Chaucer with fine artistic sense departed from this limited verse-form early in his career. He became one of the first poets to introduce into English poetry the five-beat line, and he experimented in it with a variety of rhyming combinations.

In *The Canterbury Tales*, apparently for the first time in English poetry, Chaucer used, among other meters, a five-beat, seven-line stanza, rhyming *ababbcc* (later known as the rhyme royal), for "The Man of Law's Tale," "The Clerk's Tale," "The Prioress's Tale" and "The Second Nun's Tale." A song in "The Clerk's Tale" is composed in five-beat, six-line stanzas rhyming *ababcb*; and "The Monk's Tale" is composed in five-beat, eight-line stanzas rhyming *ababbcbc*. Both of the meters were also new to English poetry. In "Sir Thopas" he used a medley of stanzaic forms. But the verse-form that he used most widely in *The Canterbury Tales* is the most famous, the five-beat couplet, later to be known as the heroic couplet.

Chaucer's versification is masterly, but it derives its effectiveness from his larger mastery of poetic creativity. A reading of Chaucer's poetry may suggest simplicity, but the sensitive reader soon realizes that Chaucer has cunningly concealed the pains bestowed upon his art. We might, in fact, apply to it the words which in the *Parliament of Fowls* he applies to the art of love: "The life so short, the craft so long to learn! The attempt so hard, so keen the victory!"

Introduction to *The Canterbury Tales*

The work was planned as a series of tales within a unifying framework, although Chaucer never finished it. This sort of structure was not new with Chaucer. In *The Golden Ass* of Apuleius, a man who has been transformed into an ass travels about, has various adventures and hears a number of stories. In Gower's *Confessio Amantis*, the priest of Venus relates to the author a series of stories. In Boccaccio's *Decameron*, a group of people who have fled to the country to avoid the Plague spend their time telling each other tales. Chaucer uses the device of a number of people telling one another stories while they travel on a pilgrimage. In Chaucer's original plan, each pilgrim would tell two tales on the way to Canterbury and two more on the return to the inn. This plan was abandoned, and Chaucer completed only twenty-two tales, although fragments of two additional tales exist.

There is one significant difference between Chaucer's framework and those of the above writers: theirs are *physically possible* — or at any rate physically *visible*. That is to say, it is possible to visualize people telling one another stories in these three situations. When we attempt to visualize Chaucer's pilgrims telling one another stories, however, we realize that his structure is artificial. If some thirty-odd people are riding horseback along a narrow road, they must be spread out over several hundred yards. It would be impossible for most of them to hear what any one of them was saying. Granted this impossibility, however, the framework of a pilgrimage is otherwise an excellent one. Pilgrims in the Middle Ages *did* tell each other stories when they gathered in the inn at night; a pilgrimage was a social event, representing for many people (especially women) their only opportunity to escape for a while from the routine of everyday life.

Although the use of a framing device was not new, Chaucer's artistic approach to it was highly innovative. Other works using this device rely either on a single speaker or, as in Boccaccio, several speakers whose relationship with the tales they tell are vague. Chaucer not only managed to produce a series of highly varied and distinctive tales, but a series of equally colorful speakers as well. In addition, there is a definite relationship between these speakers and the tales they tell, with both the speaker and the tale revealing new aspects of each other. The speakers' personalities are also explored in Chaucer's introductions to them in the "Prologue" and in the conversations occurring in the "links" between the tales. These exchanges often determine the nature and the order of the tales, creating a thematic unity that aids the framing device in holding the tales together. When the Wife of Bath introduces the question of marriage, for example, the Clerk and the Merchant follow with two opposing points of view.

Chaucer's choice of the framing device of a pilgrimage also gave him a rich source of characters. The pilgrimage had become, by the 14th century, a popular form of excursion for some (as the presence of the Wife of Bath suggests), and it included the whole spectrum of society, from Knight to Plowman. This was convenient for Chaucer, since it allowed him to bring together many socially disparate types.

The shrine of St. Thomas à Becket in Canterbury was the most popular shrine in England. Becket was the son of a London merchant, not a member of the nobility. He received a good education, and his outstanding ability recommended him to King Henry II, who appointed him Chancellor in 1155. Becket served the king faithfully, aiding him in his conflicts with the barons and the church. Henry was at this time embroiled in a power struggle with the church, which, he asserted, he had the right to tax heavily.

In 1162 Becket was "elected" Archbishop of Canterbury — that is to say, he was appointed Archbishop by Henry, who hoped thereby to ensure the subordination of the church. However, Becket was a man who did what he was paid for. Now that he was Archbishop, he began to support the claims of the church, even against the king. He opposed Henry's taxing the church, and also a royal proposal for a tax that would have fallen heavily on the common people. In 1164, Henry forced Becket to assent to the Constitutions of Clarendon, which strengthened the monarchy vis-à-vis the church; among its provisions was one affirming the right of the king to appoint prelates. However, Becket soon repudiated the Constitutions, and as a result he was forced to flee to France. His property was confiscated and he was branded a traitor.

The Pope's threat of interdiction (cutting him off from certain church privileges) eventually forced Henry to allow Becket to return to his office. Once back in England, however, the Archbishop persuaded the Pope to suspend the bishops Henry had appointed. This enraged the king. On December 29, 1170, four armed knights invaded Canterbury Cathedral and murdered the Archbishop. Becket offered no resistance. In fact, he seemed to invite martyrdom. In 1172 Becket was canonized, and his shrine soon became the goal of a multitude of pilgrims. In 1538, Henry VIII plundered the magnificent shrine and had Becket's name erased from the church calendar. Even after his death, St. Thomas continued to antagonize the monarchy.

T.S. Eliot's *Murder in the Cathedral*, although not historically accurate in all its details, captures the essence of what English people of the Middle Ages must have felt about St. Thomas. In any religion, an act of violence performed in a holy place is especially horrifying. Until recent times, a church was regarded as a place of asylum. Even the worst criminal could not be arrested if he took sanctuary in a church. The circumstances of the Archbishop's murder, then, were extraordinarily shocking to his contemporaries. Furthermore, the common people felt that he had been their champion against oppression. Consequently, it is not surprising that they flocked to his shrine, feeling that just to touch the place where he was killed would somehow make them a little better.

As the roads and inns improved through the century, pilgrimages became less dangerous and therefore, for some, less of a dedicated spiritual act. For many of Chaucer's pilgrims, the food, wine and exchange of stories was as important as any spiritual fulfilment. Chaucer gives us both aspects of the pilgrimage, the gluttony and drunkness of some of his group is contrasted with the worthiness and reverence of others. Furthermore, Becket's blood was believed to have healing properties, and the pilgrims who suffered from various ailments (the Summoner, for example, had problems with his skin) were probably embarking on the pilgrimage for health reasons as well.

NOTE: All quotations are from *Chaucer's Major Poetry*, edited by Albert C. Baugh. Prentice Hall, 1963.

Summaries and Commentaries

THE GENERAL PROLOGUE

Summary

It is spring, and the rain, the sun and the wind have encouraged new growth. Flowers are blooming, birds are singing, and people are deciding to make pilgrimages to holy shrines. Many people from different parts of England are traveling to Canterbury to visit the shrine of St. Thomas à Becket.

Chaucer, the narrator, is at the Tabard Inn in Southwark, waiting to begin his pilgrimage. Twenty-nine pilgrims arrive at the inn, and Chaucer speaks to each of them. They all agree to leave together early the next day. Chaucer begins to describe each of these pilgrims.

Commentary

The "Prologue" begins with an eighteen-line sentence that draws upon conventional details to describe both the setting and the serious nature of the pilgrims' journey. This description of the season functions in a symbolic manner, for spring is a time of renewal for both nature and man. In going on a pilgrimage to a holy place, the pilgrims express a desire for spiritual replenishment and rejuvenation.

Chaucer's first reference to himself (1.20) introduces the problem of the identity of the speaker. Some critics maintain that the narrator is Chaucer the poet *and* the man, while others argue that he is a fictitious creation who simply bears the same name as Chaucer. Perhaps the easiest resolution lies in regarding the narrator as simply another pilgrim, through whom Chaucer the poet may occasionally speak, but whose primary purpose is to reveal the average man's perception of the people and events he encounters. Indeed, the fictitious Chaucer often expresses opinions that are opposite to those held by Chaucer the poet, and he tells the two dullest tales of the journey — not what we would expect from the great English poet. It is the difference between the perceptions and opinions of these two Chaucers that creates much of the ironic tone of *The Canterbury Tales*.

The role of the narrator is basically that of an observer and recorder, and he begins his task by presenting a series of brief but colorful portraits of each of his companions.

19

The Knight

The Knight is an ideal knight who has fought all over the known world. In addition to being a skilled jouster, he is honorable and well-bred — a perfect nobleman.

Commentary

The Knight is the epitome of Christian chivalry. He has come fresh from battle to go on a pilgrimage. In fact, his tunic is still stained from the armor he has just taken off. Notice also that the Knight's clothing and equipment are plain; as a member of the true nobility, he feels no need to impress people by elegant dress. In the Middle Ages, a period of relatively fixed social classes, a nobleman could feel perfectly secure in his position, for no matter how he dressed or whom he associated with, he always remained noble. Hence the Knight can go on a pilgrimage with a group of commoners and mingle with them in perfect freedom, because he is secure in his own nobility.

The Squire

The Knight's son is a young man who dresses well and who can sing, play the flute, write songs and dance. He is also skilled in riding and jousting. Many of his brave feats have been demonstrations of his love for his lady.

Commentary

The Squire is a knight in training. His accomplishments are in both cultural and military areas. His devotion to his lady and his sleeplessness are also well-known prerequisites for the life of a courtly lover.

The Yeoman

The Knight and his son are accompanied by a Yeoman, who is their servant. Dressed in green, he carries with him all the equipment of a hunter.

Commentary

The Yeoman is skilled in practical matters, rather than such "useless" activities as the song-writing that the Squire engages in. He is an expert in military gear and probably repairs the armor and weapons of the Knight and Squire.

The Prioress

The Prioress is graceful, pretty, and careful of her appearance. She loves pretty things — as her coral beads and gold brooch indicate. She practices courtly manners. (The Middle Ages lacked most of our modern eating implements; people drank their soup from the bowl, or dunked their bread in it. The Prioress could do this so elegantly that she never spilled a drop.) Finally, she is sentimental and tender-hearted. She cannot bear to see a mouse caught in a trap, and she is devoted to her little dogs. She is traveling with another nun and three priests.

Commentary

When Chaucer the pilgrim admires anyone as much as he does the Prioress, we should immediately be suspicious. When we read the passage carefully, we see that Chaucer the poet regards the Prioress as a charming fraud. He conveys this impression by letting his persona admire her for the wrong things. Her devotion to courtly manners reveals that she is something of a social climber; she speaks French — but with an English accent! Her apparent tender-heartedness is also superficial. While she was feeding her little dogs roast meat and expensive white bread, people in England were starving, as a result of the economic problems produced by the Plague.

The Monk

The Monk is a wealthy man, owning several horses and expensive riding equipment. He loves food, hunting and fine clothes. He is fat and bald, but very easy-going.

Commentary

The Monk is another character whom Chaucer the pilgrim praises highly for the very qualities that Chaucer the poet finds somewhat less than admirable. The Monk is fond of hunting and he has no patience with the rules that confine monks to either study or manual labour. Chaucer the pilgrim agrees perfectly with this attitude.

Chaucer the pilgrim also admires the Monk's rich clothing and his hearty appetite for good food — both of which, of course, run contrary to the rule of poverty. Furthermore, the Monk wears a gold pin with a love-knot in it, which implies that he has also broken the rule of chastity. The Monk, then, is a perfect example of just what a monk should *not* be.

The Friar

Hubert, the Friar, is a merry, wanton man. He has arranged many marriages for young women — after he has made them pregnant — but he is well-loved by rich farmers and especially rich women. When he hears confession, he pays the most attention to those who give the most money. He is a good singer and musician, and he visits the taverns more than he visits the poor houses. The Friar is good at getting money from people, and he dresses very well.

Commentary

The portrait of the Friar is ironical. During the Middle Ages, many mendicant (begging) orders received charters from the Pope allowing their members to hear confessions and grant absolution within specified geographical limits; hence such friars were called "limiters." This situation put the limiters in competition with the parish priests and naturally resulted in problems between the two groups. The priests would grant absolution only after the sinner had done penance either through prayer or through labor on the parish church; the limiters, on the other hand, made absolution easy by granting it for a sum of money — on the theory that generosity is proof of repentance. Note the irony in 1.232, where men give silver to "the povre freres:" all these orders were supposed to be bound to complete poverty. Chaucer's Friar does not waste his time helping the poor (which is, of course, his duty). Rather, he associates with rich people. Chaucer the pilgrim is, as usual, quite blind to the contradiction between what the Friar is and what he should be. He calls him "this worthy lymytour" and says "There nas no man nowher so vertuous." Chaucer the poet is being ironic.

The Merchant

The Merchant is well-dressed, well-mounted and pompous in his speech — most of which concerns his success at making money. He is nationalistic for business reasons, but he is heavily in debt.

Commentary

The Merchant is a typical and timeless specimen of the business community. He always talks of his business enterprises, but he is not nearly as upright as he appears to be.

The church condemned usury, or the making of money out of money ("eschaunge" being one form of this), and merchants with money to put to work were forced to invent a devious sort of underground transaction ("chevyssaunce"), which was, in effect, lending money at interest. Hence the debt that the Merchant is in.

The Clerk

The Clerk is very thin and shabbily dressed. As a student, he spends all his money on books instead of food and clothes. Although he is learned, his speech is humble and sparing.

Commentary

The Clerk is a pilgrim whom *both* Chaucer the pilgrim and Chaucer the poet sincerely admire. The Clerk is poor. Unlike the Monk, he is thin, unlike the Friar, he is poorly dressed. In contrast to them, he exemplifies what a cleric should be. (Students in the Middle Ages were members of the clergy.) Unlike the Squire, he prefers books of philosophy to good clothing. He is completely devoted to his calling. He wants to learn, not so as to become wealthy, but so that he will be able to teach others.

The Man of Law

The Man of Law is wary, wise and discreet. His knowledge of law is extensive. Because he can recite the details of cases from many years ago, people think he is wiser than he really is.

Commentary

Chaucer does not question this lawyer's ability or his knowledge of the law. Yet the statement that the lawyer knows all the judgments since William the Conqueror is another example of Chaucer's deliberate exaggeration — we are to infer that he *talked* as though he knew them all.

The Franklin

The Franklin has a white beard and a red face, and he loves to drink and to enjoy life. He is generous and wealthy, and he loves to entertain. One of his chief pleasures is food, and he always keeps his house full of fine things to eat.

Commentary

A franklin was a commoner who had received a franchise entitling him to the ownership of land. Franklins belonged to the middle-class; they were commoners who had prospered. This particular franklin has done well in life, and he is liked by the other pilgrims.

The Haberdasher, the Dyer, the Carpenter, the Weaver and the Carpet Maker

The five guildsmen are all wearing new and expensive clothing, and their knives are mounted with silver instead of brass. Their wives enjoy being called "madame" and having precedence over other people at religious ceremonies.

Commentary

The medieval guilds resembled craft unions or small business associations rather than the modern industrial labor unions. These men belong to the middle-class and are skilled workers and small businessmen. They put on airs and try to prove that they are superior to the other pilgrims.

The Cook

The Cook is accompanying the guildsmen and preparing their meals. Although he is a good cook, he also drinks a lot and has an enormous sore on one of his legs.

The Shipman

The Shipman is something of a rascal since he steals wine and drowns anyone he takes as a prisoner. He is the master of a ship and although he is a good sailor, he cannot ride a horse very well.

The Physician

The Physician is very knowledgeable about medicine and surgery. He uses astrology to help him diagnose and cure people, and he can quote from all the medical authorities. He knows very little about the Bible, however, and though he made a lot of money during the Plague, he is reluctant to spend it.

The Wife of Bath

The Wife of Bath is a middle-class housewife. She likes to

be noticed: she wears scarlet hose and a big hat, and on Sundays her head kerchiefs weigh ten pounds. She is a very authoritative person and insists on always being first at the offering. She is in robust health.

The Wife of Bath is a woman of experience. She is fond of travel and has been on pilgrimages all over Europe and as far as Jerusalem. Furthermore, she has had a full sex life: five husbands, and apparently some lovers in her youth, although Chaucer is too tactful to go into detail about these. She is gap-toothed. (In the Middle Ages it was believed that widely spaced teeth indicated a highly sexual nature.)

Commentary

The Wife of Bath is in complete contrast to the Prioress. The Prioress tries always to be refined — for example, in her clothing — whereas the Wife is obvious and conspicuous. The Prioress imitates the ways of court, whereas the Wife is frankly middle-class. The Prioress appreciates all the refinements of courtly love, whereas the Wife is interested in simple sex. The Prioress has a delicate, beautiful face, whereas the Wife has a bold, healthy face. The two characters represent opposite poles of womanhood.

The Parson

The Parson is a good but very poor man. He gives money to the poor, and he is very devoted to his parish duties. Although he tries to win over sinners by his example, he does not hesitate to scold an obstinate sinner, whether wealthy or poor.

Commentary

The Parson is another character whom both Chaucers sincerely admire. Unlike the corrupt Friar and Monk, the Parson is a study in virtue. He practices what he preaches — for "if gold rusts, what will iron do?" Here we see expressed the medieval ideal of the obligation of nobility, the notion that the leader must set the example and that responsibility entails suffering.

The Plowman

The Plowman is the Parson's brother. He is a hard worker

and is very religious. His faith in God does not alter in bad or good times.

Commentary
The family connection between the Parson and the Plowman is deliberate since they both represent the virtues of their respective occupations. The Plowman's strong faith and his creed to treat people as he would like people to treat him are ideal Christian virtues.

The Miller
The Miller is so tough he can break any door by running at it and butting it with his head. Among his other accomplishments, the Miller is good at stealing wheat and playing the bagpipes. He is very fond of bawdy stories.

Commentary
Chaucer devotes a great deal of space to a description of the Miller's appearance. One explanation for this is that in Chaucer's time, people believed that they could judge the character of an individual by his physique.

The Manciple
The Manciple works for a law school, and it is his job to purchase the food. Although he is not as learned as the young lawyers, he is a shrewd and practical man who can outwit anyone.

The Reeve
The Reeve is a skinny man with a closely cropped beard and short hair. He manages a large estate, and he is so efficient and shrewd that he makes a lot of money. He even tricks his master by loaning him property that he already owns, while the Reeve collects the interest. Before he became a reeve, he was a carpenter.

Commentary
The Reeve is not only shrewd but dishonest. He is also very hard on those who work for him. It is important to remember that he was once a carpenter, as this becomes the basis for an argument later in *The Canterbury Tales*.

The Summoner

The Summoner is very unattractive, with a red face, pimples, boils and a scaly infection. He loves to eat pungent foods like garlic, leeks, onions and strong wines. He is lecherous, and if someone buys him some wine, he will ignore the fact that they have a mistress.

Commentary

The Summoner is a thoroughly unattractive character. Not only is he physically ugly, but he eats offensive foods. He is also a lecher, a drunk, a blackmailer and a hypocrite.

The Pardoner

The Pardoner says he has come straight from Rome with some pardons that he hopes to sell. He also has a number of fake relics, which he hopes gullible people will buy. He is a friend of the Summoner, and the two men like to harmonize on songs together. However, the Pardoner has a voice as weak as a goat's. He has long yellow hair and no beard, and he is possibly a eunuch. Much of the Pardoner's success is due to his oratorical ability — he manages to frighten everyone into giving him money.

Commentary

A pardoner was a man who had received a special charter from the Pope entitling him to grant forgiveness for sins — including future sins. With the passage of time, this practise of granting pardons, or indulgences, became more and more subject to abuse. By Chaucer's time, there was widespread corruption in the sale of indulgences.

The Pardoner is attached to the hospital of Rouncivalle, and supposedly all the money he makes goes to this hospital. From what we learn of his character, however, it seems likely that the hospital never sees a considerable portion of the Pardoner's takings.

Chaucer now apologizes for the stories he is about to relate. His excuse is that he is simply setting down what was actually said. He also apologizes for the bawdy stories that will follow.

Of course, Chaucer's apology and excuse for telling his tales is not completely genuine, since Chaucer the poet invented these characters and assigned them these tales. In effect, he is giving us here one of the few theories of literature that we have from the Middle English period. Chaucer says here that the writer's task is to tell the truth. On the other hand, most literature in the Middle Ages is written as if it were history.

The Host

The Host is a typical hostler. He is always at ease and full of good cheer — especially after the pilgrims have paid their bills. He flatters them outrageously and loudly proclaims his desire to help them in any way possible. With great gusto, he sets forth his proposal: each pilgrim shall tell two tales on the way to Canterbury and two on the way back. The best story-teller will receive a dinner at his inn when they return — a dinner paid for by the whole company. The winner will be the pilgrim who tells the tale of "best sentence and moost solass" (best moral meaning and most merry).

Early the next morning the pilgrims depart for Canterbury. After some time the Host halts the group and announces they will draw straws to see who will tell the first tale. The Knight draws the shortest straw and begins his tale.

Commentary

The Host is the one pilgrim of whose historical existence we have almost certain evidence. In the prologue to "The Cook's Tale" he is addressed as "Herry Bailly." There are records showing that a Henry Bailly did own an inn at Southwark during the period Chaucer was writing about, and a man of this name — probably the same one — was a member of Parliament in 1376-77 and 1378-79, and served as tax assessor or coroner between 1377 and 1394. So it appears that Chaucer, by putting him into the poem, was having a little fun with an innkeeper with whom he was acquainted.

THE KNIGHT'S TALE

Summary

PART 1

Old stories tell us that there was once a Duke called Theseus, who was Lord and Governor of Athens. He had conquered many countries, among them an area called Scithia. He married Hippolyta and made her his queen, and he brought her and Emily, her sister, home with him. On the way, they met a group of women clothed in black who were grieving by the roadside. They asked for Theseus' pity because their husbands had been killed during the siege of Thebes. The cruel lord of Thebes, Creon, had dishonored the bodies of these men by ordering that they not be given proper burials.

The Duke was moved by their plight, and he swore that he would take vengeance on Creon on their behalf. Ordering his wife and her sister to continue to Athens, he led his army to Thebes. Creon was killed, and the bodies of their husbands were returned to the grieving women.

Following the battle, two badly wounded warriors of Thebes, Arcite and Palamon, were presented to Theseus. They were recognized as being men of noble birth by the coats of arms they wore, and Theseus ordered that they be sent to Athens to be kept as perpetual prisoners who could not be ransomed for any price. Theseus then returned to Athens, and for the next several years Arcite and Palamon remained in the prison, grieving because they would never gain their freedom.

One day in May, a month when people feel refreshed and rejuvenated, Emily began to wander in the garden, gathering flowers to make a garland for her hair. The dungeon where the prisoners were kept was close to the garden, and Palamon, who was pacing in his cell, happened to see her from his cell window. He was so struck by her beauty that he cried out as if in pain.

Arcite immediately asked him what was wrong and warned him to be patient and try and endure the agony of their imprisonment. Palamon told him that it was the beauty of the woman he just saw that caused him to cry. He wondered if she might be Venus, the goddess of love, and he prayed that she might help them to escape. Arcite was curious then and also looked out the window. He was as moved by her beauty as Palamon was, and he swore that unless he saw her every day, he would surely die.

Palamon was greatly upset by this and accused Arcite of being a traitor. They had sworn eternal friendship and had promised never to interfere in each other's love for women. Palamon then reminded him that he was the first to fall in love with the woman and that Arcite had made an oath to help him in all things.

Arcite argued that Palamon's love was only spiritual; he himself loved her as a man loves a woman. Besides, all is fair in love, and he was not bound by oaths in this matter. Since they were both in prison, however, it does not matter if they both loved her and wanted to fight over her since neither had any chance of winning her love.

One day, Perotheus, a Duke and a boyhood friend of Theseus, came to visit him in Athens. He was also an old friend of Arcite, and he begged that he be released on the condition that he would leave Athens. Under these conditions, Arcite would be beheaded if he returned.

Arcite was released but was no happier. While he was in prison, he could at least catch a glimpse of the woman he had fallen in love with. Now he envied Palamon because he was still in Athens, and it was possible, since he was of noble birth, that he may some day meet Emily.

Meanwhile, Palamon was upset because now Arcite was free to assemble an army to conquer Athens and win the love of Emily. Both men were suffering intensely, each thinking the other was most fortunate. The Knight poses the question: who was suffering the most?

PART II

When Arcite returned to Thebes, he was intensely miserable. He declined food, sleep and the company of others, and, as a result, his appearance changed. He became pale and thin, and people couldn't recognize him.

After two years of such suffering, he experienced a vision of Mercury, a Roman god. Mercury told him that if he returned to Athens, his sorrow would end. Arcite immediately decided to follow these instructions, even if it meant that he might have to lose his life in an attempt to see Emily.

Looking at himself in a mirror, Arcite saw how drastically his appearance had changed. He decided that no one would recognize him and, disguised as a laborer, he traveled to Athens with a young attendant. He gained employment as a servant in Emily's house and lived there for several years.

Arcite, who now called himself Philostrato, was promoted because of his good manners and became Theseus' personal chamber-squire. He was well-paid, and, with the addition of money brought secretly to him by his countrymen, he became wealthy. He also became a close friend of Theseus.

In the meantime, Palamon had been languishing in prison for seven years. With the help of a friend, however, he managed to escape and hid in a field. He intended to remain hidden until nightfall, when he would return to Thebes and gather together an army to overthrow Theseus and win the hand of Emily.

That same day, Arcite rode his horse to the country to make a garland of flowers. By chance, he arrived in the same field Palamon was hiding in. Palamon didn't recognize Arcite, and Arcite didn't see Palamon. Arcite, still forlorn about his love for Emily, thought he was alone and spoke aloud to himself about his tale of misery. Palamon overheard his speech and emerged from his hiding-place to accuse Arcite of being a traitor. He declared that he was now Arcite's mortal enemy and that one of them must die. Arcite challenged him to a duel and arranged that they would meet the next day to fight to the death for Emily.

Arcite arrived with armor for both of them the next morning, and they began a furious fight. By chance, they were interrupted by Theseus, who, with his entourage, had come to the country to hunt deer. Angered by the fact that they were fighting without a referee, Theseus demanded to know who they were and what their duel was about. Palamon explained the situation to him, and Theseus had them both condemned to death.

The women who had accompanied Theseus on the hunt, including Hippolyta and Emily, begged him for mercy, and Theseus agreed to spare the two men. However, he set a condition for their freedom: Arcite and Palamon had to return in a year, each accompanied by one hundred knights. A joust would be held at that time, and, since love for Emily was the root of the problem, the winner would receive her as his wife. Grateful for Theseus' mercy, Arcite and Palamon returned to Thebes.

PART III

Theseus spent a year building a beautiful stadium for the duel. Shaped in a circle, it was a mile wide and sixty feet high. He also ordered that three altars be built in the stadium: one to Venus, the goddess of love; one to Mars, the god of war; and one to Diana, the goddess of chastity. The Knight describes each of these statues in detail.

When one year had passed, Arcite and Palamon returned to Athens, each with one hundred knights, all magnificently armed. Lycurgus, the king of Thrace, accompanied Palamon, and Emetreus, an Indian King, was with Arcite. All the men were greeted with a wide array of welcoming festivities — feasts, songs and dancing.

Palamon went to the altar of Venus before the battle and prayed for his victory over Arcite. If he couldn't win the hand of Emily, he wanted to die in combat. He left the altar certain that Venus would answer his prayer.

Shortly after Palamon had prayed to Venus, Emily went to Diana's shrine. She asked Diana to change Arcite's and Palamon's love for her. If this couldn't be done, then she hoped that the one who loved her most would be able to marry her. She then saw a vision of Diana, who promised that she would be wed to one of the two men.

Arcite then rose and pleaded at the altar of Mars, asking that he would win the battle with Palamon. Mars appeared and told him that he would win the battle.

Mars and Venus began arguing in Heaven, each having promised support for one of the two men. Saturn, the god of destiny, stopped the argument by promising that both of them would be able to assist Palamon and Arcite in the way that they had said. Palamon would win the hand of Emily, and Arcite would be victorious in battle.

PART IV

On the day of the joust, the contestants faced each other at opposite ends of the arena, all with elaborate armor and excited horses. Crowds of enthusiastic people were everywhere, placing bets on the battle and making a great deal of noise.

Theseus had the two men brought to him and had a herald tell the crowd about the rules of the joust. He wanted to avoid a battle to the death and so put restrictions on the kinds of weapons that could be used. He also declared that anyone injured in the battle would be taken to the sides of the arena. When either Palamon or Arcite was wounded or killed, all fighting had to cease. Theseus, Hippolyta, Palamon, Arcite and Emily all rode down to the arena, and the battle began.

The men engaged in a fierce bout of fighting until at last Palamon was injured, and although Palamon tried to remain in the field, he was taken to the side. Theseus ordered the battle to stop and declared that Arcite had won the hand of Emily.

The crowd rejoiced, but Venus was furious that her promise had not been fulfilled. Saturn advised her to be patient, and as Arcite rode around the arena in triumph, Saturn caused his horse to throw him. Arcite, badly injured, was taken to Theseus' palace.

Theseus then returned to Athens. He was well-pleased with the outcome of the fight since no lives had been lost, and he was certain Arcite would live. He ordered that festivities should continue for three days and presented the knights with gifts before they left on their journey home.

Even though Arcite was surrounded by doctors, his condition worsened. He sent for Emily and Palamon, and he expressed his eternal love for Emily. He told them both that he knew no better man than Palamon and advised Emily to consider him as a prospective husband.

After Arcite died, Emily grieved deeply, as did all the people of Athens. His body was burned on a special funeral pyre built on the command of Theseus in the field where he and Palamon had first fought for the love of Emily.

After many years had passed and the mourning for Arcite had lessened, Theseus sent for Palamon and Emily. He informed them that, following the decree of Jupiter, the king of the gods, he has decided that "after grief, there should be bliss." Emily had his permission to marry Palamon, and they were married that same day. They lived a happy life together, with no sorrow or jealousy in their marriage.

Commentary

The Knight begins the story-telling with a tale of chivalric romance. His tale of Palamon and Arcite combines the traditions of medieval romance and classical epic, though the ancient type is more apparent in the title and structure of the Italian original, Boccaccio's *Teseide*, or epic of Theseus. The classical forerunner of both poets was Statius, the author of the *Thebaid*, whom Chaucer, somewhat misleadingly, cites as a source. In "The Knight's Tale" he chooses to claim ancient authority for his medieval fiction, but in all the essentials of the story he actually follows the *Teseide*. Even in characterization, in which he usually showed independence, he departs very little from Boccaccio.

"The Knight's Tale" is a very different poem from its Italian source. In the first place it is only about a quarter as long as the original. At the outset Chaucer strikes his pace and passes over in a dozen swift lines the campaign of Theseus against the Amazons, to which Boccaccio devotes his whole first book. And he continues to hasten the development of Boccaccio's very leisurely narrative. Nevertheless he finds room for significant additions of his own. Only about a third of the English poem is actually translated from the Italian, and some of its most memorable features — the descriptions of the temples, the account of the tournament, the passages of philosophical reflection — are in large part independent of the *Teseide*. By adapting both action and setting to the life of his time, Chaucer made the tale more real and vivid. Its pervading humor, too, he greatly heightened, so that some critics have been led, unjustifiably, to pronounce "The Knight's Tale" a satire on chivalry or courtly love.

"The Knight's Tale" is highly stylized, concerned not with real people but with the ideas by which people in the real world live by. Emily, for example, is not very convincing as a real woman. It is rare for her to actually do anything within the story, and when she does act, she acts according to people's expectations. She begs for the lives of Palamon and Arcite when they are first discovered fighting in the field. She welcomes Arcite as her husband and then mourns his death for years, but she is still able to live a happy life with Palamon. In all her actions and in her appearance, she represents the ideal love toward which all knights aspired.

The portraits of the two knights are not very individualized either. We are informed by the Knight that this is a simple story about rivalry in love, and thus we are encouraged to take the side of one or the other. Yet Arcite and Palamon are similar in their feelings and actions, and when Arcite dies, we are not altogether convinced that justice has been served.

The question of justice or Fate, however, is a central one in "The Knight's Tale." When Palamon wins the hand of Emily in the end, it is less a triumph of justice than a suggestion that Fate moves in strange ways, and people must try, as Theseus points out, to "make a virtue out of necessity."

Finally, "The Knight's Tale" is not only about ideal or courtly love, in which a knight is prepared to go to any lengths to win the affection of his beloved, but it also includes other aspects of chivalry. Arcite's and Palamon's deep devotion to one another represents the "comradeship in arms" that is a central quality of courtly life, and a sense of honor pervades much of their behavior.

THE MILLER'S PROLOGUE

Summary

When the Knight finishes his story, everyone, especially the "gentlefolk," agree that it is a "noble" story. The Host wants the Monk to follow with a similar kind of tale, but he is interrupted by the Miller. The Miller, who is quite drunk, argues that he has a "noble" story to tell, and, although the Host attempts to persuade him not to, he insists upon being heard.

After he states that he is going to tell a tale about a carpenter, the carpenter's wife and a student, the Reeve objects, saying that it is not right to speak of scandals. The Miller assures him that most wives are virtuous, but he wants to tell the story of one who wasn't. Chaucer the pilgrim apologizes to us for including this story, which he feels we may find crude, but reminds us that there are plenty of other stories in *The Canterbury Tales* that will please more refined minds.

THE MILLER'S TALE

Summary

There was once a rich old carpenter who lived in Oxford. He took in a lodger named Nicholas who was a student of the arts but who had become interested in astrology. One of the things Nicholas had learned was how to forecast rain. Nicholas was a notorious lover who took advantage of his meek and youthful appearance. He decorated his room with herbs and fruit and spent his nights playing a harp.

Not long before this, the carpenter had married Alison, a pretty young woman, and he was devoted to her. However, he was very jealous, since he was so much older than her, and he kept a close watch over her. One day when the carpenter was out, Nicholas embraced her and pleaded that he was in love with her. Although Alison protested, she was eventually convinced of his love and promised that she would meet with him when she could. She warned him of her husband's intense jealousy, but Nicholas was sure they could find a way to trick him.

A while later, Alison left the house to go to church. In this church there was a parish clerk named Absalom who, among other things, was a fancy dresser, a good dancer and a musician. He was, however, a bit prim and squeamish about people who expelled gas in public. As he passed the collection plate, he admired many of the parish women, but it was Alison with whom he was falling in love.

That night, he went to Alison's house with his guitar and sang her a love song underneath her window. The carpenter asked Alison if she had heard him and although she answered that she had, she didn't say how she felt about it.

Absalom became quite miserable since Alison didn't seem to be responding to his wooing. He tried a number of different approaches, sending her gifts of wine, food and money, but all he got in return was her scorn. She was in love with Nicholas, and she ignored Absalom, thinking he was a fool.

One day Nicholas and Alison agreed that they would play a trick on the carpenter that would enable them to spend the night together. He took enough food and drink to his room to last for a couple of days, and Alison agreed that she would say she didn't know where he was if her husband asked about him.

After a couple of days, the carpenter began to wonder what had become of Nicholas and sent his serving-boy up to his room to see if he was there. The serving-boy looked through a hole in the door and saw Nicholas sitting staring into space. When the carpenter heard this, he was afraid Nicholas had had a fit and they broke down the door to his room. When they finally succeeded in rousing Nicholas, he told them he had discovered, through the use of astrology, that rains would begin to fall on the next Monday, and that a flood would occur, worse than the one that Noah had experienced in Biblical times. All mankind would be drowned in one hour. The carpenter, fearing that Alison would be drowned, begged to know if there was anything they could do to save themselves. Nicholas told him of a plan that would ensure their survival. The carpenter had to get a tub for each of them and hang them from the roof. They would also need food and an axe to cut the ropes holding the tubs when the waters began to rise. In addition, they couldn't say anything while they were in the tubs, and the tubs had to be hung far apart from one another.

After he told his wife (who pretended not to know of the plan), the carpenter got the tubs, hung them on a beam of his roof, and filled them with food and drink. On the night the flood was to occur, the carpenter, his wife and Nicholas got in their tubs and prayed. After a short while, the carpenter fell asleep, exhausted by the work of getting the tubs ready. While he was sleeping, Nicholas and Alison got out of their tubs and went to bed together.

At the same time, Absalom discovered through some friends that the carpenter had not been seen for a while and had probably gone away for a couple of days to pick up some lumber. Thinking that Alison was alone, he decided to go to her house to tell her of his love and to get a kiss from her.

Just before daybreak, Absalom dressed in his finest clothes and went to the carpenter's house. He called for Alison from underneath her window, asking her for a kiss. She tried to send him away by telling him that she loved another. But Absalom was convinced that she cared for him and insisted that she kiss him. Alison agreed, on the condition that he leave immediately after.

Alison then told Nicholas about Absalom, and they decided to play a trick on him. She extended her rear end out the window, and, because it was still too dark to see, Absalom kissed it, thinking it was her lips.

Absalom was furious when he discovered that he had been tricked and vowed revenge upon Nicholas, whom he had overheard talking in Alison's bedroom. He woke up the blacksmith and asked to borrow a poker that was red-hot from resting in the fire. Returning to the carpenter's house, he called for Alison, asking for another kiss. This time, Nicholas put his rear end out the window. Absalom then asked Alison to speak so that he could tell where she was, and, in response, Nicholas expelled gas. Although Absalom is nearly blinded by the blast, he manages to hit Nicholas in the rear end with the hot poker.

Nicholas cried out in pain for water, which woke the carpenter from his sleep. The carpenter, thinking the flood had started, cut the rope on his tub and fell to the floor. Alison and Nicholas began to scream "Help!" and "Murder!" causing the neighbors to run to their aid. When they arrived, they found the carpenter had broken his arm, and Nicholas and Alison told them he had gone crazy and had thought that Noah's flood was coming a second time. All of the neighbors laughed and ignored the carpenter's attempts to explain, and everyone in the town agreed that he was insane.

Commentary

"The Miller's Tale" is the first example of the fabliau in *The Canterbury Tales*. By definition, fabliaux are short, bawdy tales, with quick-moving plots. The placement of this tale, following as it does "The Knight's Tale," is central to our enjoyment of it. Not only does its lightness and quick pace pick us up from the slow-moving tale it succeeds, but it complements "The Knight's Tale" with its strange mixture of indecency and courtly love.

Like "The Knight's Tale," this story involves the wooing of a beautiful young woman by two young men. Although Alison is obviously very different from the pure and idealized Emily, she is described in the same courtly language when we first hear of her. In fact, one of the most striking humorous devices Chaucer manipulates in this tale is the use of phrases drawn from the language of courtly love. The sense of justice or destiny that becomes somewhat difficult to accept in "The Knight's Tale" emerges again in an entirely different manner. Justice, in this tale, is simplified — the carpenter deserves to be duped because he has married a woman far too young; Absalom deserves to be duped because he is so foolish and meek; and Nicholas deserves to be duped because he has deceived the carpenter. Perhaps Alison's actions are repaid by having this bawdy tale told about her.

In telling this tale, the Miller has been true to his character as we saw it in the "General Prologue." He has also been true to his promise of "repaying" the Knight for his tale, since he makes fun of the notion of courtly love that "The Knight's Tale" takes so seriously.

THE REEVE'S PROLOGUE

Summary

Although some people make various comments upon "The Miller's Tale," most of the pilgrims laugh. Osewald, the Reeve, however, is a little upset since he is a carpenter. He is also middle-aged and resents the Miller's negative description of the older carpenter and his young wife. Though older men cannot do all the things they once could, he says, they can still lie and boast.

The Host urges him to get on with his story, reminding him that they haven't time to waste on personal sermons. The Reeve warns the pilgrims that his story is told in response to the Miller's story, and it will therefore use the same kind of rough language.

Commentary

The Reeve has taken the Miller's story as a personal insult — he is a middle-aged carpenter himself. His tale is devised to pay the Miller back for what he sees as an attack upon himself. The most effective way of doing this, of course, is to tell a tale about a miller.

THE REEVE'S TALE

Summary

There was once a miller who lived in Trumpington, not far from Cambridge. He enjoyed life and could do many things: play the bagpipes, fish, fix his equipment and poach deer. But he was also a bully, and he stole corn and meal from people who brought their grain to his mill. Since he was a big man and carried a large knife, however, no one dared to fight him. His wife was well-bred, and, being the daughter of a parson, she had been educated by nuns. They would often walk together, the miller a few steps ahead of his wife. Although she was probably illegitimate, no one made fun of her for fear of her husband.

They had two children, one a girl of twenty and the other a baby boy. The girl was very attractive, and the parents were especially concerned that she only be wooed by men of good breeding.

The miller charged a great deal of money for grinding grain, especially for the wheat and malt brought to him by a large college at Cambridge. One day, the man from the college who usually came with the grain to oversee the miller's work was too sick to come, and the miller took advantage of his absence by stealing outrageously. Later, when confronted by the angry warden of the college, the miller simply denied that he had cheated them.

There were two students at the college, John and Alan, who came from a village in the north. They had heard of the miller's trickery and convinced the warden to let them spend a morning watching the miller grinding their grain so that the college wouldn't be robbed. They loaded some corn upon a horse, went to the mill and told the miller they wanted to watch him work.

The miller suspected the two students and decided that he would rob even more than he usually did to prove that just because they were scholars, they were not necessarily wise. When the students weren't looking, he untied their horse, which promptly ran off to join some wild horses nearby.

After the corn was ground and put in sacks, John and Alan discovered that their horse was gone and ran off to catch it. While they were gone, the miller emptied half of the flour from their sacks.

By the time the students were able to capture their horse, it was dark and too late to go back to the college. When they asked the miller if they could spend the night with his family, he made fun of them by saying that though his house was small, scholars always made things seem bigger than they are. They decided to stay, however, and the miller sent his daughter into town to get them some bread and ale. The miller cooked a goose for supper and tied the students' horse up. He also made up a bed for them. The house was so small that they would have to sleep in the same room as the miller and his family.

During supper, everyone drank a lot of ale, especially the miller. After everyone went to sleep, John and Alan lay awake, trying to think of ways to get revenge upon the miller for stealing their flour. Alan decided to avenge himself by sleeping with the miller's daughter, and so he quietly slipped into her bed and did just that.

Meanwhile, John was still awake, somewhat angry that Alan had received the benefit of their plan for revenge. When the miller's wife got up to relieve herself of the ale that she had drunk, John moved the baby's cradle from the foot of her bed and placed it next to the bed he was sleeping in. When she returned to the darkened room, the miller's wife mistook John's bed for hers since she felt the cradle there, and she got into bed with him. Like Alan and the miller's daughter, John and the miller's wife enjoyed themselves.

As dawn approached, Alan said goodbye to the miller's daughter. She told him where the miller had hidden the flour and suggested that they should take it as they leave. Alan went to the bed where John was sleeping but, discovering the cradle, thought he had gone to the wrong bed. He got into the miller's bed instead and, thinking he was speaking to Alan, he proceeded to tell the miller of the night he has just spent with his daughter. Furious, the miller began to curse and fight with Alan.

The noise woke up the miller's wife and, thinking that her husband was in the bed beside her, she jumped out of bed and hit her husband with a stick because she mistook him for one of the students. John and Alan then hit the miller a few more times, took the flour that was stolen from them, and made their way back to the college.

The Reeve suggests that the moral of the story is "do evil and be done by as you did." He hopes that he has repaid the Miller on the pilgrimage with this story.

Commentary

Once again, we have a bawdy tale and, once again, a tale involving a certain form of justice. Just as all the characters in "The Miller's Tale" got their just desserts in the end, so too the cheating miller, with his inflated sense of pride in his wife and his daughter, and with his bullying ways, is punished by two people he has wronged. He has both cheated the students and tried to make fun of their scholarly ways. In return, they retrieve the stolen goods, as well as humiliating and beating up the miller.

Like "The Miller's Tale," this tale falls into the genre of the fabliau. The practical joke central to the plots of most fabliaux is here, as is the somewhat indecent subject matter and the brevity of the narrative. The tale is well-suited to the Reeve, who is, as we have seen in both the "General Prologue" and the prologue to this tale, a sullen man. Although it is a fabliau and therefore, by nature, a comic tale, "The Reeve's Tale" also contains evidence of the Reeve's sense of bitterness and anger toward the Miller on the pilgrimage.

THE COOK'S PROLOGUE

Summary

Roger, the Cook, has obviously enjoyed "The Reeve's Tale." He thinks the miller got what he deserved for trying to embarrass the students. He announces that he will tell a story that actually happened in his town. The Host interrupts and jokingly warns the Cook that he must tell a good tale to make up for all the stale pies he has sold them. The Cook then proceeds to tell his tale.

THE COOK'S TALE

Summary

There was once an apprentice cook living in Roger's town. He was known as Perkin Reveler because he was an accomplished dancer and loved to have a good time. Whenever there was a wedding, he would sing and dance, and he would rather visit the tavern than tend the shop. Perkin also loved to gamble and used to join in with processions of people to find others to gamble with.

His master finally caught on to Perkin's behavior and realized that he was never in the shop when he was supposed to be. He remembered an old proverb: "throw out a rotten apple from the hoard or it will rot the others," and decided to fire Perkin so he wouldn't influence the other apprentices.

After this, Perkin himself decided to follow an old proverb: "birds of a feather flock together," and moved in with a young man as fond of revelry as himself. This friend's wife kept a shop, but only to disguise her immoral activities.

Commentary

"The Cook's Tale" exists only as a fragment. Scholars differ in their opinions as to why Chaucer never completed it. Some maintain that Chaucer felt that three "bawdy" or merry tales in a row upset the balance of *The Canterbury Tales* and therefore decided to abandon this one. After all, in the Host's original plan, the tales were supposed to be of both "sentence" (edification) *and* "solass" (merriment).

However, even in its fragmentary state, this tale is an amusing story of a careless young man. It also represents

42

another example of how proverbs provided the moral of the story in many of the tales popular in Chaucer's time.

INTRODUCTION TO THE MAN OF LAW'S TALE

Summary

The Host notes that the day is passing quickly and reminds the pilgrims that they must not waste any more time. Once time is gone, it is gone forever. He then turns to the Man of Law and, using the language usually found in legal documents, he requests that the Man of Law fulfill his contract to tell a tale. The Man of Law replies — also using legal language — that although he promised to tell a story, Chaucer the poet has already told all the good stories in existence in his many books. There are no tales left for the Man of Law to tell. After listing many of Chaucer's works, the Man of Law also points out that Chaucer writes in rhyme, which he is not able to do. He will tell a story, even though it will not be as poetic as those of Chaucer's.

After spending the first night of their pilgrimage at Dartford, the pilgrims have had a late start on the second day of their journey. The Host is concerned about the passage of time. Already a quarter of the day has passed, and no tales have been told. The reader must remember that the Host is in charge of the tale-telling contest, and the pilgrims must speed up their pace if all the tales are to be completed within the duration of their pilgrimage.

THE MAN OF LAW'S TALE

Summary

PART I

A group of wealthy, serious and wise merchants once lived in Syria. They had a prosperous business, trading in spices, fine fabrics and many other items. They decided to go to Rome to see if any opportunity for trade existed there. While they were in Rome, they came to hear of Constance, the daughter of the Emperor. She was well-known for her beauty, goodness and innocence, and she was well-loved by all the common people. They felt that with all her fine qualities, she was the model of a perfect woman.

When the Syrian merchants returned home, they were eagerly greeted by the young Sultan of their country, who was interested to hear of their journey. Among other things, the merchants spoke a great deal about the wonderful Constance.

After hearing about this beautiful and virtuous woman, the young Sultan was convinced that he wanted her for his wife. He summoned his councillors and informed them that if he could not have this woman for his wife, he would surely die.

The councillors foresaw a number of difficulties. There were different laws and customs in the two countries. It was not appropriate for a Christian country to form an alliance through a royal marriage with a country that worshipped Mahomet. To this the Sultan replied, "I would rather be baptized than lose the Lady Constance." Eventually, the Sultan and all of his subjects became Christians.

Constance was to be his bride, and in Rome, the Emperor made elaborate preparations for the journey to Syria. Just as they were about to leave, however, Constance grew pale and grieved because she was being forced to leave her home and her friends to go and live in a strange nation. Even so, she set off on her journey without even the benefit of an astrologer's advice as to when the best time to travel was.

Meanwhile, the Sultan's mother began to conspire with some councillors against her son and his wedding. Her son was forcing her to give up her religion so that he could marry a Christian and this angered her. She told the councillors that she would prefer to die rather than forsake Mahomet. They all agreed amongst themselves that they would pretend to convert to Christianity until the climax of the feast, whereupon they would attack the visiting Romans. The Man of Law concludes this section of his tale by attacking the treachery and wickedness of the Sultan's mother.

PART II

When the Christians arrived in Syria, they were received with great celebrations, and they began the overland journey to the Sultan's palace. Even the Sultan's mother joined the crowds that went to greet them. On the day of the wedding, there was a great feast that was attended by all the Syrians and many Romans. In the middle of the banquet, the confederates of the Sultan's mother swarmed into the hall and killed everyone, including her son, since she desired to be ruler of Syria. The only one who was not killed was the Lady Constance. She was given food and drink and was forced aboard a boat and cast upon the sea. She sailed for many days and underwent many frightening experiences until one day she came upon a northern land called Northumberland.

Here there was a castle, and the constable of the castle discovered the wreck of Constance's boat. Even though they couldn't understand each other's language, he took her into his home, and he and his wife cared for her. They were both pagans, but Constance was true to her Christian faith, and, before long, the couple also became Christians. Most Christians had fled that part of the country when it was invaded by pagans, but some Christians remained and practised their faith in secrecy.

However, Satan was keeping a close watch on Hermengild, the constable's wife, and he was eager to repay her for converting to Christianity. One night, Satan (disguised as a knight) entered the constable's home and killed Hermengild. When the constable returned, he discovered the knife in Constance's hand, put there by the knight. The constable took Constance to see Alla, the King of Northumberland, who was a wise and powerful ruler. After the king had heard what had happened, he asked her to defend herself. Constance dropped to her knees and prayed to God to protect her.

Alla was moved by Constance and ordered that the knight be brought before him. Only if the knight would swear upon an oath that Constance killed Hermengild would Constance be executed. The knight came forth and upon a Bible he swore that Constance had killed Hermengild. He was immediately struck dead, and a voice said that he had unjustly accused a Christian. That heavenly visitation awed the court, and the king and many of his subjects were converted to Christianity. Shortly after, Alla married Constance and there was much rejoicing. However, Donegild, Alla's mother, did not take part in the celebration. She was furious that her son would dishonor his country by marrying a foreigner.

While the king was at war with Scotland, Constance gave birth to a boy and a message was sent to Alla. This message was intercepted by Donegild, who substituted a letter claiming that the child was horribly disfigured.

When the king received this false message, he accepted the misfortune as God's will and sent this message home. Donegild was furious when she heard this, and, once again, she substituted a false letter. This letter said that Constance and the child must be cast upon the sea in a boat.

After the letter arrived, Constance obeyed the command, since disobedience would be punished by death. She boarded the ship with her son and some supplies, and they sailed away.

PART III

When the king returned from the war and heard about his wife and his son, he was stricken with grief. He recognized the handwriting in the false letter, however, and his mother was executed for her crime.

Meanwhile, Constance's boat was beached near a heathen castle. Many people gathered around to look at her and her child, and the steward from the castle boarded the ship. He tried to force her to sleep with him, but the Virgin Mary intervened and Constance was saved. The steward was swept over the side of the boat and into the sea.

The Emperor of Rome had, by this time, heard of the slaughter of the Romans by the Syrians, and he sent an army to Syria to seek his revenge. After they had slaughtered the Syrians, the army began to journey home. A Senator who was leading the army came upon Constance in her boat and brought her and her son back to Rome with him. Constance had lost her memory and did not recognize her homeland.

Alla had been grieving over the loss of his wife and child for some time, and he decided to make a pilgrimage to Rome to make penance for what had happened to Constance. He was well-received in Rome, and many people came out to greet him, including the Senator. After a few days, he asked that the Senator meet with him again, and the Senator arrived with Constance's son. When Alla saw the child, he inquired after his background. He was struck by how closely he resembled Constance, and so he asked that he be allowed to visit the Senator at home to meet the boy's mother.

When Alla saw Constance, he was overjoyed and explained to her how they had both been deceived by false letters. Alla and Constance rejoiced in their reunion, and Constance then presented herself to the Emperor as his daughter. Later, Constance and Alla returned to Northumberland.

Unfortunately, Alla died within a year, and Constance went back to Rome with her son, Maurice, who eventually became Emperor.

Commentary

Although the Man of Law claims to have heard this tale from a merchant many years ago, Chaucer's source for the tale was the Anglo-Norman prose *Chronicle*, written by Nicholas Trivet in the 14th century. The basic plot of the story was fairly common, however, and there were many tales circulating around that time involving a heroine who is persecuted by some evil person (in this case, her mothers-in-law), suffers exile and many hardships, but is eventually seen to be innocent of all charges and is reunited with her family. That her persecutors are punished by either God or man is an essential element in the development of the moral message of the tale.

The story of Constance is a story of "sentence," or moral teaching. Such stories were common in the Middle Ages, and they provided a way in which Christian virtues could be exemplified in the lives of individuals.

Although "The Man of Law's Tale" has many elements of the "fabulous" — foreign lands, astrology and the mysterious and dramatic deaths of the knight and the constable's wife, for example — it is, above all, a Christian story. Constance embodies Christian humility, hope and faith. She is, as her name suggests, constant in her devotion to God, and she moves through many desperate and life-threatening situations with the protection of God.

THE MAN OF LAW'S ENDLINK

Summary

After the Man of Law finishes his tale, the Host congratulates him for telling such a good story. He reminds the Parson that he had promised them all a tale and calls upon him to tell a story as excellent as the one the pilgrims have just heard. The Parson, however, is taken aback by the Host's swearing. When the Host begins to make fun of the Parson's prudish manner, the Shipman interrupts and offers to tell a tale.

Commentary

This link, which exists only as a fragment, is sometimes referred to as the "Epilogue" to "The Man of Law's Tale." It also serves as an introduction to "The Shipman's Tale," although some scholars feel that "The Wife of Bath's Tale" was meant to be the next tale. Some of this confusion can be traced to the fact that what is now "The Shipman's Tale" was originally given by Chaucer to the Wife of Bath, although he later changed his mind and created another tale for her. The order of tales in this study note is that as found in Albert Baugh's, *Chaucer's Major Poetry*.

The exchange between the Host, the Parson and the Shipman is a good example of how Chaucer manages to infuse the links between the tales with drama and humor. The Host evidently feels that it is time for a serious tale and wants the Parson to provide it. However, his swearing is totally inappropriate and suggests that perhaps he doesn't want to hear a serious tale after all. When he insists that the Parson "preach" to them, the Shipman breaks in and argues that the Parson will preach heresy. The Shipman, however, is not as concerned about the religious content of the tale as he is that he may be bored by a sermon of any kind. He offers to tell a tale himself because he is in the mood for bawdiness and mirth. Even though the Host is in charge of the contest and it is up to him to decide the order of the tales, he allows the Shipman to proceed. The Host also seems to be fond of the less serious tales.

THE SHIPMAN'S TALE

Summary

There was once a merchant from St. Denys who had a beautiful wife. He was as generous as his wife was pretty, and he often entertained people from different social levels.

One of his frequent guests was a monk — a handsome young man who was about thirty years old. The merchant and the monk became close friends. Indeed, the monk convinced the merchant that they were cousins, since they were born in the same town. The merchant never questioned this but instead vowed to treat the monk as if he were his brother. In turn, the monk was generous to the merchant's servants, tipping them well each time he visited, and so became a guest welcomed by all in the household.

One day, the merchant began preparing for a business trip to a place near Bruges, where he hoped to buy some wares. He invited the young monk to stay with his family for a day or two before he left. The monk agreed, and he arrived at the merchant's house with gifts of food and drink.

On the third day of the monk's visit, the merchant woke up early and went up to his counting-room to try and figure out the financial state of his business. In the meantime, John, the monk, went for a walk in the garden. There he saw the merchant's wife, and, noting that she looked tired, he jokingly suggested that her husband had kept her awake all night. The wife told him that this was not true. In fact, her life was so miserable, she had often thought of killing herself.

The monk encouraged her to "unfold her grief" to him, arguing that talking about her problems may make her feel better. He also thought that he might be able to offer some advice or help. He vowed that he would not repeat anything that she told him. The wife then told the monk about the marital neglect that she had suffered from her husband, even though she was reluctant to criticize a man who was so closely related to the monk.

At this, the monk exclaimed: "He's no more a cousin to me than this leaf hanging on the tree!" He had only told the merchant they were cousins so that he would be able to see more of her, the woman he loves.

The wife then told John that her husband's worst fault was his stinginess, and she asked John to lend her one hundred francs so that she could buy some new clothes. John was sympathetic and promised to bring the money to her after her husband left on his trip. Before they parted, the monk kissed her passionately.

She then went up to call her husband for dinner and chided him for ignoring his guest. The merchant explained that a man in his complicated business had to work hard to earn a living. He asked her to take good care of the household while he was away and warned her to be thrifty with the money he has left her since she already had all the clothes she needed.

After supper, John wished the merchant well on his trip and asked him, in secret, if he would lend him one hundred francs so that he could buy some cattle. The merchant agreed but warned John that money is essential for a merchant's business, and he would therefore have to pay back the loan as soon as possible.

The merchant left for Bruges the next day. Shortly after, the monk returned to the merchant's house. The merchant's wife agreed to spend the night with him in return for a gift of one hundred francs.

When the merchant returned home from his trip, he realized that the wares he had bought had cost so much that he was now in need of money. He decided to go to Paris to borrow from some friends, and while he was there, he stopped by to visit John. He hadn't come to collect the money he had lent, but when he mentioned his financial troubles, John told him that he had already repaid the loan to the merchant's wife.

The merchant left for home in a good mood, since he had made some clever business arrangements in Paris. When he reached his house, he chided his wife for not having told him that John had repaid the loan. His wife immediately answered that while the monk had given her some money, she had thought it was a gift and had spent it on clothes. She was angry with the monk for having let her believe that the money was a gift and asked her husband to forgive her. The merchant realized that there was no point in arguing any more, and he forgave her. He warned her, however, that she must be more economical in the future.

Commentary

In tone, "The Shipman's Tale" lies midway between the two extremes represented by "The Knight's Tale," which is in the style typical of courtly love poetry, and the Miller's and Reeve's tales, which are bawdy. "The Shipman's Tale" is certainly not courtly, like the Knight's; but neither is it as coarse as the Miller's. We might classify it as "good clean fun about sex." "The Shipman's Tale" is not as vivid as the Miller's, but far more vivid than the Knight's. It conveys much of its ribaldry indirectly, through imagery that carries a double meaning.

From the introductory lines, it is clear that Chaucer originally intended that this story be told by a woman, probably, as suggested earlier, the Wife of Bath. In 1. 1202, for instance, the Shipman refers to himself as if he were a woman. Nevertheless, the tale suits the character of the Shipman, since he is obviously a hearty man who enjoys a bawdy story. Also remember that as a Shipman, he would have encountered many merchants and would likely have had some cause to want to make fun of them.

John's speech to the wife is full of lecherous insinuations, conveyed largely through imagery. The picture of the weary, frightened hare suggests the sexual inadequacy of the husband; sex and fear are as incompatible as sex and humor. This image subtly contradicts the suggestion which follows, that the husband has been "laboring" his wife all night. By implication, John is reinforcing his original statement, that a real man needs only five hours of sleep at night.

Paradoxically enough, when John makes his declaration of love, he swears on his profession. This can be interpreted in either of two ways: he may mean his profession as a monk — which of course demands chastity; or he may mean the profession of faith that he made when he became a monk — which includes a vow of chastity. By either interpretation, then, it is an inappropriate way to swear his love.

As soon as John has promised to lend the wife a hundred francs, he begins taking liberties with her. This incident shows Chaucer's psychological shrewdness; when the man has done the woman a favor, he can hardly wait to take advantage of her.

THE WORDS OF THE HOST TO THE SHIPMAN AND THE PRIORESS

Summary

The Host congratulates the Shipman on his tale and wishes him good luck. He criticizes the monk in the tale for his deception of both the merchant and his wife.

Looking around for the next story-teller, he suddenly changes the tone of his speech and addresses the Prioress in a polite manner, requesting that she tell the next tale.

Commentary

The Host reacts to "The Shipman's Tale" in his usual way, wih great gusto and a dirty joke of his own. He addresses the Shipman as "gentil maryneer" — an odd title for a man who, as we know from the "General Prologue," likes to drown his enemies.

THE PRIORESS' PROLOGUE

Summary

The Prioress calls upon God and the Virgin Mary. She first praises God's power and magnificence, and then she states that she will tell her tale in honor of both God and the Virgin Mary.

She asks the Virgin Mary for help in telling her tale. The Prioress claims that she is not a good speaker and doubts her ability to tell the other pilgrims about the Virgin Mary.

Commentary

The Prioress begins her tale with an invocation to the Virgin Mary. This is an understandable way for her to begin; the Virgin was an important figure in medieval catholicism, and a nun would be likely to identify with her. The invocation also fits the character of the Prioress as Chaucer has described her: she is somewhat pretentious and therefore begins her tale very formally. Note that she expressly praises the Virgin's humility. The Prioress is anything but humble. Here we have another example of a Chaucerian character lauding something which she is not capable of being.

THE PRIORESS' TALE

Summary

In Asia, there was once a Christian city that had a Jewish quarter. This "ghetto" was not closed off, and anyone could walk through it.

There was a Christian school at one end, and a young Christian boy used to run through the ghetto to attend his classes. He was only seven years old and the son of a widow. This boy loved the Virgin Mary, and he used to kneel in front of any likeness of her that he saw.

One day in school, the boy heard the older children sing the *Alma redemptoris*. Even though he did not understand the Latin, he vowed to memorize the hymn so that he could sing it in honor of the Virgin Mary on Christmas Day. In the days that followed, the boy walked through the ghetto practising the hymn.

Meanwhile, Satan whispered to the Jews, telling them that it was a disgrace that a boy be allowed to sing such a hymn where they live, thus spiting the faith and laws of Jews.

After this, the Jews began conspiring, and they tried to come up with a way of ridding themselves of the young Christian boy. They finally decided to hire a murderer. This man waited in an alley for the boy to pass by, jumped upon him, slit his throat, and threw his body into a cess-pit.

All that night, the boy's mother waited for her son to return. When morning arrived and he had not yet come home, she went to the school and learned that he was last seen in the ghetto.

She searched all over the ghetto, asking after her son, but they all said they had not seen him. However, Jesus led her to the pit, and she discovered her son's body.

Suddenly, the dead boy miraculously began to sing the *Alma redemptoris*. The Christians, amazed by this miracle, formed a procession and carried his body to the abbey. The leaders of the Christians then tortured and killed all the Jews who had conspired to kill the boy.

While a monk was preparing the boy — who was now considered a martyr — for burial, he asked him how he could sing when his throat had been slit. The boy said that even though his throat was cut and he should have died, the Virgin Mary had spoken to him as he was dying and had laid a grain upon his tongue. He would be able to sing until that grain was taken away, at which point she would return for him. When the monk removed the grain, the boy's spirit left his body, and they buried him in a marble tomb.

The Prioress concludes her tale by praying that Hugh of Lincoln, a child similarly murdered by Jews, will pray for the sinful people of the earth.

Commentary

This tale is a medieval type called a "Miracle of the Virgin." Such stories recounted instances in which the Virgin miraculously aided someone who had been devoted to her.

The school the young boy attends is a typically church-oriented grammar school, teaching students to read Latin and sing. "Doctrine" here means "What was taught," not specifically church dogma, and the Prioress seems to feel that nothing more than the ability to read well enough to go through the services, and the ability to sing the anthems, is required of the devout and pious student. This idea is reinforced by her apparent feeling that the boy's song in honor of the Virgin is sincere, even though he doesn't understand the meaning of its words. There is, of course, another way of looking at this: that it is the spirit of the deed, rather than its nature, which determines its worthiness.

Note that the monk who comes to bury the boy's body receives special comment, the Prioress observing that he was a holy man, "As monkes been — or elles ouhte be." This is clearly a reference to the sly and adulterous monk of the preceding tale and to the Host's comments on monks in her Prologue. Whether it is also directed against the Monk among the pilgrims is a more difficult question to answer.

The Prioress' religious attitude is revealed by the "grain" which the Virgin places on the boy's tongue to enable him to sing after his throat is cut. Precisely what this word means here — whether the seed of some plant associated with the Virgin, a piece of consecrated wafer from the Mass, or precious stone (the pearl was a symbol of Mary) — is uncertain. However, it is treated here as a magic object like those found in many pagan fairytales, and its use as a device reduces the miracle from the realm of the sacred to the superstitious. Surely, the Virgin is thought of as capable of giving speech to the dead; no "gimmick" is needed to perform the act.

When one compares this tale with the rest of Chaucer's own work, or even to most surviving medieval writings, one receives the impression that it entails more cruelty than most, and certainly more than *any* of Chaucer's. Beyond any question, the Prioress dwells unnecessarily on the degrading treatment of the child's corpse. This emphasis on filth and degradation is far more repulsive than the Miller's earthy grossness or the Wife of Bath's hearty obscenity. Similarly, the Prioress' description of the torture which included being pulled apart by wild horses and the hanging of all who had any knowledge of the crime, seems vicious and tasteless — hardly in keeping with the surface appearance of Madam Eglantine. Although criticial opinion is not unanimous, it seems reasonable to interpret Chaucer's choice of this tale for the Prioress as a deliberate revelation of her failings as a religious figure.

PROLOGUE TO SIR THOPAS

Summary

The pilgrims are quiet after hearing about the miracles in

"The Prioress' Tale," and, once again, the Host begins to joke. He turns to Chaucer and teases him about his habit of looking at the ground. He then makes fun of Chaucer's physical appearance. He wants a tale of mirth, and Chaucer, afraid that he will appear stupid, says that he only knows one rhyme.

Commentary

The religious tale of miracles has touched all the pilgrims — even the most loud-spoken and bawdy ones — and the Host wants to relieve the tension it has created. The butt of his humor is Chaucer the pilgrim. If the Host can convince such a shy and quiet person to tell a tale of mirth, the effect on the pilgrims will be much greater.

The reader should remember, however, that the shyness of Chaucer the pilgrim is probably intentional. He is not a timid man, or he would not have spoken to all the pilgrims at the Tabard Inn and made friends with them so quickly. If he has been quiet while on this journey, it is because he is listening carefully to all the tales. Remember that he has taken upon himself the task of memorizing these tales, so that he may relate them at a later time.

CHAUCER'S TALE OF SIR THOPAS

Summary

There was once a young knight called Sir Thopas. He lived far across the sea in Flanders. His father was a lord of high degree who controlled a great deal of land.

Sir Thopas was a handsome man who dressed in fine clothes. He was a skilled hunter, archer and wrestler. All the young woman in that country spent their nights thinking about him. But Sir Thopas was a chaste young man, and he took no interest in women.

One day as he was riding in the forest, the songs of the birds made him think of love. Tired of riding, he stopped for a while to rest himself and his horse. He dreamt that he slept with an Elf-Queen and upon waking he decided that he would search for as long as it took to find such a queen.

Once in fairy-land, he met a three-headed giant called Olifaunt who ordered him away. The Queen of Fairies lived there, and no one could enter. Sir Thopas said that he would meet the giant the next day for a duel. He then returned home to prepare himself for the fight. Musicians and story-tellers entertained him, servants brought him food and drink, and others helped him with his armor and weapons.

Chaucer tells the pilgrims that although there have been many tales of romance told over the years, the tale of Sir Thopas will emerge as the best story of them all.

Commentary

The irony in the words between the Host and Chaucer continues in "Chaucer's Tale of Sir Thopas." Although the Host criticizes the quality of this tale, it is in fact a skilfully drawn parody. Throughout the tale, Chaucer uses well-known clichés and absurd speech.

The tales that Chaucer is satirizing in the "Tale of Sir Thopas" were popular in medieval times, and they were roughly the equivalent of today's "pulp" fiction. These tales all followed the same basic plot: a handsome young knight encounters many adventures while trying to win the hand of a fair maiden.

Like the tales he satirizes, "Chaucer's Tale of Sir Thopas" is full of lengthy descriptions and unlikely situations. One of the more subtle ways in which Chaucer parodies these pulp romances is by depicting his knight — the symbol of manhood — as an effeminate man. His appearance and manner seem to more closely resemble that of a fair maiden than that of a hearty young nobleman ready for battle.

THE LINK BETWEEN SIR THOPAS AND THE TALE OF MELIBEE

Summary

Just as Chaucer is beginning the second part of his tale, he is interrupted by the Host, who orders him to stop at once. He has had enough of Chaucer's "illiterate rhymes." Chaucer protests that he is doing the best he can, but the Host insists that he is merely wasting their time and asks him to tell a tale in prose instead — either a tale of mirth or one with a wholesome moral. To avoid an argument, Chaucer agrees to tell a little tale, but he warns the Host that it will contain morals that they have heard before in other tales.

Commentary

An interesting aspect of this exchange is that it suggests that Chaucer the poet was trying to emphasize the fact that he is not Chaucer the pilgrim. For instance, the Host attacks Chaucer the pilgrim for the poor quality of his poetry, yet Chaucer the poet was, of course, recognized as one of the greatest poets in the English language. This helps to lend a tone of ironic humor to the link, but it also reminds us that Chaucer the pilgrim was a fictional character, not to be confused with the actual author of *The Canterbury Tales*.

CHAUCER'S TALE OF MELIBEE

Summary

In this moral debate, or dialectical homily, Dame Prudence, the wife of Melibee, is the main character. Other friends of Melibee, however, also offer their opinions. Melibee himself occasionally states his point of view, but he is always convinced of the "correct" view in the end.

While Melibee was away from home, his daughter, Sophie, was attacked and wounded by three robbers. The main subject of the debate was whether violence should be punished by violence. Various aspects of revenge were discussed and debated, including: how to clean one's heart of anger; how to tell true friends from false ones; whether women can be trusted; whether women's advice should be followed; whether private revenge is justified; and the importance of reconciling oneself to God.

The robbers were then brought before Dame Prudence, who suggested a peaceful settlement. Naturally, the robbers were delighted. Melibee decided that a fine was sufficient punishment and was persuaded by his wife to forgive the men.

When the three men were brought before him, Melibee does forgive them but also points out that he is being generous towards them and criticizes their behavior.

Commentary

Because of its length and its serious tone, this tale is often not included in otherwise complete versions of *The Canterbury Tales*. Chaucer translated the essay from a French tale, *Le Livre de Melibee et de Dame Prudence*, a work which in turn had been translated from a Latin essay by Albertano called *Liber Consolationis et Consilii*. This kind of tale was popular in Chaucer's time, but it is unlikely that he originally made the translation for *The Canterbury Tales*.

THE MONK'S PROLOGUE

Summary

The Host is pleased with "Chaucer's Tale of Melibee," particularly with the patience of Dame Prudence. He wishes his wife had heard the tale, since whenever he is in a fight with someone, his wife urges him to continue the violence. Even though the Host is a hearty man, he cannot stand up to his wife's shrewishness.

He then turns to the Monk and tells him that it is his turn to tell a story. He jokingly wonders why a virile-looking man like the Monk ever decided upon a religious vocation.

The Monk agrees to tell a few tales of tragedy. Such tales concern high-ranking people who lost their power and glory and are usually told in six-foot lines called *exametron*.

Commentary

Here the Host suddenly reveals himself to be a henpecked husband, married to a shrewish woman who bullies him constantly. Typically, when he turns to make his selection of the next teller of tales, he makes bawdy and suggestive jokes, almost entirely of a sexual nature. Notice as well that once again the Host is concerned about the passing of time — they have almost reached Rochester, and he tells the Monk not to "hold up our game."

THE MONK'S TALE

Summary

Although Lucifer was an angel and therefore not subject to the whims of fortune, he fell through sin. Likewise, Adam had a beautiful existence until one action caused him to lose everything.

Sampson was a great ruler of Israel, and he had been given tremendous strength. His treacherous wife convinced him to tell her the secret of his strength and then betrayed him by relating it to his enemies and taking another husband for herself. His enemies learned that his hair was the source of his power, and they blinded him, cut his hair and threw him in a cave. One day, his enemies wanted to make fun of him and asked him to display what strength he had. But Sampson's strength had returned, and he destroyed an entire temple, killing his enemies and himself. The Monk says that the moral of the story is that men should not reveal secrets to their wives.

Hercules was another famous man of great strength and courage who traveled throughout the world killing ferocious animals. He fell in love with a beautiful woman, Deianira, and she made him a beautiful shirt. But poison was woven into the shirt, and when he put it on, he began to die. Hercules did not want to die from poison, so he threw himself on a fire. Beware the subtle tricks of fortune is the moral of this tale.

King Nebuchadnezzar had a great store of treasure, which included gems taken from Christian temples. He had conquered Israel and ruled over its people. Daniel was one of his subjects, and he had the gift of understanding dreams. One day the king had a golden statue made and commanded that all must bow before it. Daniel and his two friends refused. Nebuchadnezzar was cast down from his throne by God, who forced him to live among animals. When his punishment was over, he had recognized the ultimate power of God, and he had realized that no earthly king could be His equal.

Nebuchadnezzar's son, Balthasar, inherited the throne from his father. He did not follow the warning given to his father, and he worshipped idols instead of the Christian God. He and his family boldly drank wine from sacred Christian vessels to honor his own gods. As a result, his kingdom was overthrown and he was killed.

There was once a Persian queen named Zenobia who was beautiful and courageous. As a young girl, she had gone off into the woods and had become a skilled huntress. She was also very strong and an accomplished wrestler.

Zenobia married Prince Odenake and although they were happy, their marriage was flawed by one thing. She slept with him only until she became pregnant, and then she refused to share her bed. In this way, they had two sons.

Together, Zenobia and Odenake conquered many lands. One day Prince Odenake was killed. Zenobia then ruled alone, and she was cruel to her enemies. A Roman leader named Aurelian, however, finally conquered Zenobia and brought her back to Rome where she was jeered at by crowds of people.

A number of famous men have been the victims of treachery and betrayal. King Peter of Spain was killed by his own brother, King Peter of Cyprus was killed by his companions, and Bernabo, Visconti of Lombardy was betrayed by his nephews and was killed in prison.

Count Ugolino of Pisa was imprisoned in a tower with his three children, the oldest of whom was only five years old. A bishop had circulated lies about him and had arranged that he and his children would receive little food or water. One day the food stopped arriving, and after a while, one of his children died. Eventually, the other two children also died of starvation, as did Ugolino himself.

These were a few examples of how mighty and powerful men have been betrayed and destroyed.

Nero was a powerful man who ruled over many lands. He enjoyed his wealth and was inclined toward excess in everything he did. He had the city of Rome burned just for his amusement, had people killed just to hear the sounds of their pain, slept with his sister and killed his brother. He even had his mother's body cut open so that he could see the place where he was born.

One night, the Roman citizens rebelled against Nero, and he could find no friend who would protect him. In desperation, he killed himself rather than face torture and death at the hands of the mob.

There has never been a captain as powerful as Holofernes. He forced the entire world to give up their religions and worship only King Nebuchadnezzar. One night when he had fallen asleep after drinking, however, he was killed by a woman named Judith.

King Antiochus was an arrogant and evil man who thought that there was nothing that he couldn't do. He hated the Jews, and he attempted to destroy them. God prevented him by causing him to have terrible pains in his body. But Antiochus persisted, so God caused him to fall from his chariot, and he became crippled. God then filled his body with parasites so that he gave off an odor so foul that no one would go near him. His final punishment was a painful and lonely death.

No one could match Alexander for power and fame. He was so victorious in battle that he conquered the entire world. Eventually, however, he was betrayed and poisoned by his own people.

Julius Caesar became the greatest conqueror in the world, even though he was of humble birth. Brutus, who was envious of Julius, conspired aganst him. As Julius walked up to the Capitol one day, Brutus and the other conspirators stabbed him to death. Even though Fortune may seem to be man's friend, she is not to be trusted because she often turns against man.

Croesus, King of Lydia, was condemned to die by fire, but a sudden rain saved his life. This made him foolhardy because he thought he was protected in some way. He had a dream, and his daughter warned him that it foretold his death. He ignored her warning and was hung.

Commentary

"The Monk's Tale" is based on Boccaccio's *De Casibus Virorum et Feminarum Illustrium*, which relates the downfalls of various famous persons. Boccaccio's book is one of the great works of the early humanism of the Italian Renaissance.

Renaissance humanism meant an emphasis on the Greek and Latin classics. The humanistic scholars studied these classics, and the humanistic writers tried to convey classical ideas in the writings of the time.

The humanist emphasized the importance of man as an entity in himself; this concept contrasted with the medieval view that a man was worth studying only if he had done something extraordinary. Boccaccio's *De Casibus* displays this Renaissance interest in man in a general way. Chaucer more or less brings the work back to the Middle Ages by cutting out everything but the bare essentials, so that we have left only short accounts of the downfalls of famous persons.

We have noted that where Chaucer has assigned a story to a particular character, it is either just what we would expect from that character or just the opposite of what we would expect. We would never expect the gay, worldly Monk to relate a series of tragic stories, but he assures us that he has a hundred tragedies to tell.

Of further interest in "The Monk's Tale" is that most scholars agree that Chaucer had once decided to write a book of tragedies much like Boccaccio's collection. He apparently abandoned this project and decided to assign many of these stories to the Monk. Although the inner sections of "The Monk's Tale" were not arranged chronologically, they do represent an early attempt of Chaucer's to write a series of tales before he conceived of *The Canterbury Tales*. These tragedies also represent what one critic has called "the orderly habits of medieval literature."

THE NUN'S PRIEST'S PROLOGUE

Summary

Before the Monk can begin another tale of tragedy, the Knight interrupts and begs him to stop. Even though he enjoys hearing the occasional tale of someone of wealth and power who is struck down by bad luck, he prefers to hear stories of happier events.

The Host agrees, saying that the Monk has begun to bore them with his stories. He reminds the Monk of an old proverb: it doesn't matter what you say if you have lost your audience. He asks the Monk to tell them a tale about hunting instead.

The Monk declines, and the Host then asks the Nun's Priest to cheer up and tell them a tale. The Nun's Priest agrees and says he will try to tell them an amusing story.

Commentary

The interruption of "The Monk's Tale" provides us with an intriguing glimpse into the dynamics of the pilgrims. Even though these somewhat tedious tragedies are boring everyone, the Host, usually the first to reveal his displeasure with a tale, is reluctant to stop the Monk because the Monk is of a higher social class. It is therefore up to the Knight, someone of even higher social standing, to bring the tale to a halt. Only then does the Host criticize the Monk and request a change in topic.

THE NUN'S PRIEST'S TALE

Summary

A long time ago, a widow and her two daughters lived in a small cottage near a meadow. They led a simple life with very few possessions and barely had enough to get by on. The widow had a rooster that she called Chauntecleer. This rooster was a wonderful crower — he sounded better than any other rooster, and he knew the time by intuition. He was also a beautiful bird, brightly colored and well-kept.

Chauntecleer was in charge of seven hens. One of them,

Pertelote, was especially pretty and gracious. Chauntecleer had loved her since she was only seven days old.

One morning, Pertelote was awakened by Chauntecleer, who was groaning as if from a bad dream. When she asked him what was wrong, he told her that he had just had a terrifying dream of an animal that tried to kill him. From the way Chauntecleer described him, the animal in his dream was a fox.

Pertelote was ashamed of him for being afraid of a mere dream. How could she love someone who displayed such cowardice? She was sure the dream was caused by an excess of "red choler" in his blood and reminded him that Cato had said that dreams meant nothing. She suggested that he take a laxative to purge himself so that the dream would not recur. She even offered to help him select the herbs for this preparation.

Chauntecleer thanked Pertelote but went on to point out that despite what Cato said, he had read many old books where authorities on the subject claim that just the opposite is true. In fact, they have proved that dreams can be accurate premonitions of both good and bad things that will happen to people.

As an example, he related the story of two friends who, while on a pilgrimage, reached a busy town. They could find nowhere to stay together, so they reluctantly separated and went off to find individual accommodations. The first one was able to stay in a stall with some oxen and the second one found a place to stay elsewhere. Later that night, the second friend had a dream in which his comrade told him that he would be murdered in an oxen stall. The young man ignored the dream, even though he dreamt it twice. His friend appeared to him in a dream a third time and told him that he had been killed and robbed. He also told him that the next day his body would be hidden in a cart full of dung. The second friend went to find his comrade the next day and, as his dream had indicated, he found his friend's body. The murder was revealed and the murderers were executed.

Chauntecleer then told of another example of a dream that was a premonition. Two men, waiting for good weather before beginning a boat trip, spent a few days in a seaside town. The winds finally changed and after deciding to leave the next day, they went to bed early. One of them dreamed of a man who warned him that if they sailed tomorrow, they would be drowned. He tried to talk his friend out of going, but the friend decided that dreams were nonsense, went by himself and was subsequently drowned.

Chauntecleer cited several more examples of the importance of taking note of dreams. When Saint Kenelm was only seven years old, he foresaw his own murder in a dream. Others, such as Daniel and Joseph of the Old Testament, Croesus, King of Lydia, and Andromache, Hector's wife, had dreams that foretold important events.

On the basis of such evidence, Chauntecleer argued, he was not in need of a laxative. But he didn't want to offend Pertelote and told her that when he looked at her loveliness, all his fear vanished. After all, "woman is man's delight and all his bliss." With this, he woke up the rest of the hens and spent his day the way he usually did.

Meanwhile, a fox who had lived near the farmyard for three years broke into the yard where Chauntecleer lived and hid in a cabbage-bed. This was the fox that Chauntecleer had dreamed about.

Chauntecleer had followed Pertelote's advice about a laxative and was walking around the yard, looking for herbs. While watching a butterfly, he happened to see the fox. Frightened, he would have fled except that the fox told him not to be afraid. He claimed he meant no harm and that he had only come to listen to Chauntecleer's singing. He said he could only remember hearing such a beautiful voice once before, and that voice had been Chauntecleer's father's. He asked Chauntecleer if he would sing so that the fox could tell if he really was better than his father.

Such flattery worked on Chauntecleer, and he closed his eyes and began to sing. The fox immediately leapt upon him, grabbed him by the neck and carried him off into the woods.

The hens began to make a terrible noise, shrieking and yelling in fear and dismay. The widow and her two daughters ran out into the yard to see what was causing the commotion and saw the fox running away with Chauntecleer. Soon the family and all the farm animals were pursuing the fox, yelling and making a great deal of noise.

Chauntecleer feared for his life, and he suggested to the fox that he should yell back at his pursuers. Without thinking, the fox decided to do just that and opened his mouth to shout some insults. Chauntecleer immediately escaped and flew up into a tree.

Once again, the fox tried to lure Chauntecleer with flattery and promises, but the rooster had learned his lesson. He would not allow his vanity to get him into such trouble again!

Commentary

"The Nun's Priest's Tale" has always been one of the most popular pieces in *The Canterbury Tales*. Its dramatic structure (of which the many digressions and asides are all part) is excellent. The characters of the cock, the hen and the fox are vividly alive both as animal actors in the little drama and as representative human attitudes. The moral of the tale is simple — keep your eyes open and your mouth shut — but Chaucer's treatment is rich in suggestive and ironic overtones concerning the relation of the sexes, the dangers of pride, the pretensions of knowledge and human frailty in general.

"The Nun's Priest's Tale" has a long literary tradition behind it. It is based on the convention according to which people, or at least recognizably human characteristics, are presented in the guise of animals. It is convention which goes back at least to Aesop, a Greek slave who lived about 600 BC, nor does it end with Chaucer and the Middle Ages. La Fontaine used the form in the 17th century, John Gay in the 18th and in our time George Orwell's *Animal Farm*, and animated cartoons in general are evidence that the representation of human qualities in animal form has a universal imaginative appeal.

Chaucer's immediate models in the genre were the beast epics or beast fables that were popular in Europe in the 12th and 13th centuries. In situation and event the French beast fable is nearly identical with "The Nun's Priest's Tale." The difference lies in the subtle touches Chaucer introduces, and in what he adds by way of emphasis and elaboration.

In all previous versions of the story the animals are stock figures, but Chaucer makes them sharp, though tolerant, satiric portraits. The comedy arises from the variety of ways in which Chaucer allows us to see the characters. Chauntecleer polices his little yard with imposing authority. He is "roial . . . as a prince in his halle", and this, of course, is the way Chauntecleer sees himself. We see him this way as well, for the moment, but Chaucer continually returns his heroic figure to the real world of the farmyard with some passage of realistic observation, as when Chauntecleer crows or when he forages for food.

Chaucer oscillates subtly between Chauntecleer the hero of a near-tragedy, and Chauntecleer whose "tale is of a cok, as ye may heere". The ironic implication is clear enough: is a barn-yard rooster the only being who may sometime see himself in this heroic way? His mate, the "faire damoysele Pertelote," is given her own individuality. She is the affectionate but fussy spouse. The contrast between the two makes the discussion of dreams into a delicate domestic comedy. Pertelote, as one might expect, takes a practical, down-to-earth view of Chauntecleer's dream of the fox. She had read enough medieval physiology to know that a dream of a red beast indicates an excess of red choler in the body. The medication is simple enough: a laxative. No man likes to have his dreams dismissed as easily as this, and Chauntecleer is no exception.

The fox is sharply delineated as a character. As the villain he is, of course, "ful of sly iniquitee", and Chaucer gives him the disarming civility and social polish traditionally associated with villainy. He is visibly dismayed by Chauntecleer's suspicion — "Be ye affrayd of me that am youre freend?" — and protests his innocence. He goes straight to his victim's weak point, which is his pride in his singing. After references to the angels in heaven, and to the philosopher Boethius (who wrote a treatise on music) the fox produces an irresistable argument in favor of Chauntecleer's giving a demonstration: could he be as good as his famous father? Chauntecleer lifts his beak, shuts his eyes and the trap is sprung.

Another source of comedy in "The Nun's Priest's Tale" is Chaucer's use of the mock heroic or mock epic mode. All comedy relies, in some way, on disproportion or incongruity, and in mock heroic writing the incongruity is between the "grand style" commonly associated with epic poetry, and the lowly or trivial subject matter. Chaucer uses several of the conventions and techniques of epic writing in his farmyard fable. The description of Chauntecleer at the beginning is deliberately inflated and grandiose, suggesting the heroes of epic and romance.

EPILOGUE TO THE NUN'S PRIEST'S TALE

The Host congratulates the Nun's Priest on his "merry tale of Chauntecleer." Once again, he makes joking comments about women, and he suggests that if the Nun's Priest had not entered the church, he would have been a very popular man among women.

THE WIFE OF BATH'S PROLOGUE

Summary
The Wife of Bath begins by asserting that she has always trusted experience to reveal the truth about life. She has had a great deal of experience in marriage, having been married five times, and this has taught her that marriage is a misery. There is nothing wrong with having five husbands, however, even though Jesus once spoke harshly to a woman who had been married five times. Instead, the Wife of Bath follows the biblical command to "go forth and multiply." After all, Solomon had many wives, and St. Paul said that it is better to marry than to burn.

She cannot recall a time when the Bible commands virginity. It may be advised for those who seek perfection, but the Wife of Bath is not perfect. Also, if everyone were virgins, who would sustain the human race? The sexual organs weren't created just to tell men and women apart — they were created for reproduction and pleasure. She intends to sleep with her husband whenever he wants her to, and she suggests that men should show the same courtesy toward women.

The Pardoner interrupts, saying that while he was just thinking of getting married, he is now having second thoughts after listening to the Wife of Bath. She tells him that she has barely begun, and he will soon hear of all the problems men and women have. The Pardoner begs her to continue, and the Wife of Bath agrees, adding that she hopes her views won't offend anyone.

Of her five husbands, three were good and two were bad. The three good ones were rich and old. It isn't always easy to get a man, but she had these husbands eating out of her hand. This is how she controlled her first three husbands. A talented woman can always prove that her husband is at fault. When her husbands would complain about her extravagance, the Wife of Bath would accuse them of eyeing other women. As a general rule, women can also hide their faults from their husbands until after they are married. She argues that husbands should not keep the worth of their possessions a secret from their wives and that they should trust their wives, letting them go where they please. In short, the Wife of Bath gained control over her husbands by pointing out all their faults to them and by saying that because they were so flawed, they were not fit to judge her conduct. She was so accomplished at this ploy that her husbands usually ended up apologizing for things they hadn't done every time they attempted to complain about her.

Her fourth husband, however, was different. Even though the Wife of Bath was young and full of life, this husband kept a mistress. This made her furious, so she devised a plan of revenge. Although she was not actually unfaithful to him, she let him think she was, and he felt some of the same agony she had felt.

When this husband died, she married for a fifth time. Although this fifth husband, Jankyn, was the worst, he was the one she married for love and not for wealth. She had met him while her fourth husband was away on a trip, and he had suggested that if she should ever become a widow, he would marry her even though she was twice his age.

After they were married, they began to argue. He tried to stop her from visiting her friends, but she was stubborn and refused to follow his commands. Jankyn was a clerk, and he used to enjoy reading stories of "wicked wives" and quoting proverbs critical of women to the Wife of Bath. In fact, he even collected all the terrible things ever written about women and put them in one large book. One night in particular, he began to read aloud to her about famous evil women throughout history. This infuriated the Wife of Bath and she ripped some pages out of the book and hit him in the face. He then struck her so badly that he was afraid he had killed her.

There were many battles between them, but eventually Jankyn gave in to the Wife of Bath and let her run the household. She even went so far as to burn his book. After this, they lived in harmony.

Commentary

The Wife is most fully revealed in her prologue, which is a long, rambling account of her five marriages, sometimes vulgar, sometimes spiteful, sometimes hilarious, sometimes sad, but always interesting. It leaves an overall impression of a woman who has lived her life as fully as possible without regret, and with an insatiable appetite for the pleasures life has to offer. In an age in which literature exalted idealism and otherworldliness, she is happily and frankly committed to this world, and where the clerics on the journey to Canterbury argue for spirituality (often hypocritically) she argues for the delights of the senses. Five husbands are not enough — "Welcome the sixte whan that evere he shal!"

THE WORDS BETWEEN THE SUMMONER AND THE FRIAR

Summary

When the Wife of Bath finishes speaking, the Friar says that she has related an awfully long prologue for her tale. The Summoner then attacks the Friar for "butting in" and accuses him of spoiling their fun. When the Friar promises to tell a funny tale about a summoner, the Summoner says he knows many nasty tales about friars. The Host calls a halt to the argument and tells the two men to let the Wife of Bath continue with her story.

The argument between the Friar and the Summoner is intriguing for a number of reasons. It adds the kind of dramatic conflict that enlivens *The Canterbury Tales*, and it expands the personalities of these two pilgrims. Furthermore, this exchange indicates the kinds of tales the two men will later tell, and the reader will enjoy discovering just how much of their threats they intend to fulfill.

THE WIFE OF BATH'S TALE

Summary

In ancient times, when Arthur was king and when England had fairies and elves, a knight was returning to court. He saw a young woman walking by the river, and he raped her.

This act enraged a great many people, and they asked the king to condemn the knight to death. However, the queen begged the king to be merciful, and he decided to let her determine the knight's fate. She sent for the knight and told him that he would be spared if he could answer this question: "What is the thing that women desire most?" If he couldn't answer right away, she would give him a year to discover the answer.

The knight searched everywhere and asked everyone he could find. The answers varied greatly. Some said that women desired flattery, others said freedom. Other answers ranged from fun and pleasure to wealth. No matter who he asked, he always seemed to get a different answer.

The year he had been granted was over, and the unhappy knight realized he would never find the answer to the question. As he rode home, he suddenly saw twenty-four women dancing in a clearing. When he approached them to ask them the question, however, they vanished. All that was left was an ugly old woman.

The old hag asked the knight what he was looking for, and he told her his problem. She told him that she would give him the answer — thus saving his life — provided that he would promise to do anything she asked of him. The knight promised and they both went to confront the court.

When they arrived, the knight told the queen and the many women she had gathered as judges that he had found the answer to her question. He told her that what women desire most is sovereignty over their husbands. None of the women disagreed with the answer, and the knight was acquitted.

The old woman then told the queen that she had provided the knight with the answer and that he had promised to do anything she wanted. With the queen and her court as her witness, the old woman demanded that the knight marry her. Although the knight tried desperately to change her mind, she insisted and he was forced to marry her.

After a private and joyless wedding the next day, the couple went to bed. The unhappy knight tossed and turned but was unable to fall asleep. When the old woman asked him what was wrong, he replied that her age, ugliness and low breeding disgusted him.

The old woman began to lecture the knight. She pointed out that true gentility was not to be found in appearances but in virtue. Though she is lowly bred, she is still more genteel than he. As far as poverty goes, it is an admirable situation. Christ himself was poor, and authorities always say that poverty will help to lead a person to salvation.

She answered his complaint about her age by reminding him that age is supposed to win respect from people. Also, although she is ugly, he has the advantage of knowing that she will remain faithful to him and will not be courted by other men.

The knight gave in to her arguments and said she could make the choices for both of them. Since the old hag had "won the mastery," she asked the knight to kiss her. She promised that he would find her both "fair and faithful as a wife." When he turned to kiss her, he discovered that she had suddenly been transformed into a young and beautiful woman. They lived happily ever after because, as the Wife of Bath points out, the knight had allowed himself to be governed by his wife.

Commentary

"The Wife of Bath's Tale" belongs to what scholars have christened the Marriage Group because these tales all deal with the problem of how to attain happiness in marriage. The Wife of Bath says that the wife should have sovereignty over the husband; the Clerk says that the husband should have sovereignty over the wife; and the Franklin says that husband and wife should deal with each other as equals.

The Wife's tale is designed to illustrate the point she has made in discussing her life: that women desire power over men. There is no specific source for this tale, but similar stories are found in many countries. The one closest to this story is "The Wedding of Sir Gawain and Dame Ragnell," in which Gawain is saved by an old hag and has to marry her. Chaucer's version probably derives from an old Irish folk tale.

We have noted that lack of chastity was not considered particularly bad in the Middle Ages. Hence it may seem strange that the knight is condemned to death for raping a lady. The explanation is that he was attached to the court of King Arthur, and it was a special mission of King Arthur's knights to rescue ladies in distress. Damsels whose virtue was being menaced by a dragon, a giant or a dwarf would resort to King Arthur's court, where a knight would volunteer to rid them of the monster. The knight of this tale, then, in raping a virgin, was doing the opposite of what he was supposed to. (If she had been a peasant, no one would have paid any attention.)

The queen and her ladies take up the knight's cause, even though he has been guilty of an offence toward a woman. This is ironic; there are no instances in history of anyone with a reputation as a ladies' man being brought to punishment by women.

71

Of particular interest is the old woman's lecture on true nobility and gentility. The knight chides her for being ugly and old and of low descent. She then proceeds to give him a lecture on true nobility. Nobility, she says, has no connection with birth, wealth, or age; it is given by God and is not inherited. These highly unmedieval ideas are taken from Dante's *Convivio*. Chaucer, generally so typically medieval in his attitudes, advanced this theory of Dante's because he admired Dante's writings. However, because Chaucer was writing for the medieval English nobility, he put his sermon into the mouth of a ridiculous old woman, so that his audience would not feel it had to take it too seriously.

This story represents a sort of wish-fulfilment for the Wife of Bath, because the old woman gets exactly what the Wife has always wanted: a husband who is young, handsome, noble, brave, rich — and obedient.

THE FRIAR'S PROLOGUE

Summary
When the Wife of Bath finishes her tale, the Friar suggests that although much of what she has said is interesting, the quoting of authorities should be left to preachers. The pilgrims' tales are supposed to be told for fun.

He offers to tell a tale about a summoner. As he goes on to criticize the lifestyle of summoners, he is interrupted by the Host, who tells him to change his subject. The Summoner, however, says the Friar may go ahead with his tale, since he has a tale about a friar that he would like to tell later.

Commentary
The words of the Summoner and the Friar remind us that neither has forgotten the argument they had just before the Wife of Bath began her tale. Even though the Friar tells the Wife of Bath that the tales are not supposed to be serious, his tale is obviously not told simply for fun. His unkind description of summoners warns us that his tale will be a deliberate attack on the Summoner on the pilgrimage.

THE FRIAR'S TALE

Summary
There was once an archdeacon in the Friar's district who

was good at finding out what sins had been committed. The sin that he punished the most was lechery, and the people that he fined the most were those who had not given a lot of money to the church.

A summoner who worked for the archdeacon had organized a group of spies — some of them prostitutes — who would tell him who had sinned in his parish. (Here the Summoner interrupts angrily, but the Host tells the Friar to go on with his story). The summoner made a lot of money for himself through bribery and blackmail.

One day when the summoner was on his way to extort money from a poor widow on false charges, he met a well-dressed young yeoman. When the yeoman asked him what his profession was, the summoner lied and said he was a bailiff. The yeoman said that he, too, was a bailiff. Since the yeoman was a stranger from the far north, he asked if he could travel with the summoner. Since they would be traveling together, they agreed to become partners and split their profits with each other.

They began to talk about being bailiffs, and the yeoman said that he could barely cover his expenses. The summoner said it was the same for him and suggested that they switch names. At this point, the yeoman revealed that he was in fact a devil, one of Satan's agents, and that his yeoman's outfit was only a disguise.

The summoner was surprised that the devil disguised himself, but the devil explained that it was necessary in order to carry out his business. When a devil tempts a man, the man either resists temptation and is saved, or sins and is destined for Hell.

Even after being told who the yeoman really was, the summoner still agreed to keep his word and honor their partnership. Soon they came upon a farmer whose cart was bogged down and who was swearing at his horses, calling upon the Devil to take them away. When the summoner told the devil that he could have the horses now, the devil explained that he could not because the farmer did not really mean his curses. Sure enough, as soon as the horses pulled the cart free, the farmer began to bless them.

The two men then arrived at the widow's home, and the summoner explained that he was going to bribe her, even though she committed no sins. The summoner told the widow that he had an order for her to go to the archdeacon and answer for her sins. She answered that she was too ill to go and asked what the sins were. When the summoner said that he would acquit her for twelve pence, she refused to pay and said "may the Devil take you." The devil then asked her if she really meant her curse, and she said that she did, unless the summoner repented. When the summoner refused to repent, the devil took him, body and soul, to Hell.

The Friar ends his story by warning everyone to pray to Christ and thus ward off Satan. As for summoners, the Friar hopes they will repent before they go to Hell.

Commentary

No specific origin is known for this tale, but its basic theme, that of the heartfelt curse, appears in many stories. The idea is that the devil will take whatever is given him, but the giver must be sincere in the offer.

The excellence of the story lies in the imagery and the irony with which Chaucer adorns this simple plot. The story is organized around one central image, that of the hunter and the hunted. Other symbols of note are the north, which stands for Hell, and green, which indicates evil spirits or the Devil. Chaucer's subtle use of imagery adds another level of meaning to the story, and makes possible extensive use of irony.

The theme of the hunter appears in lines 1323-1326. The use of the image of the hawk (1. 1340) is also significant, since a hawk was a bird used to hunt other birds.

That the yeoman is dressed in green is important. Green was a normal color for a yeoman's clothing, but it is also a color associated with evil spirits. Hence we are given a hint that this is no ordinary yeoman. In fact, the irony in the story lies in the fact that we realize the yeoman is a devil well before the summoner does, and that we can predict the summoner's fate while he is ignorant of it.

The summoner, ashamed to admit his occupation, claims to be a bailiff. The yeoman says he is a bailiff also — which is true, since he may be considered a bailiff from Hell. The image of the hunter recurs when the summoner is compared to a *wary-angle*, or shrike (1. 1408). In the Middle Ages, the shrike was believed to kill its prey by impaling it on thorns; hence it represents symbolically a sort of religious executioner.

The ensuing conversation is highly ironic. The yeoman says that he lives in the north country (which, we know, means Hell), and adds that when he gets to know the summoner well, he will take him home and keep him there. When the yeoman admits that he is a devil, we know that he is telling the truth, but the summoner thinks this is a joke. The devil explains that he takes whatever shape will be most likely to gain his prey. The meaning of this is lost on the summoner.

We now know what is going to happen to the summoner, and we derive enjoyment from seeing him get what he deserves. This ironical situation is humorous only because the summoner is a ridiculous and evil person. If he were a sympathetic or an admirable man, the irony would be tragic. In other words, a painful situation is tragic or comic depending on whether or not we identify with the participants.

THE SUMMONER'S PROLOGUE

Summary

The Summoner is so angry with the Friar that he stands straight up in his stirrups. He says he will repay the Friar for his "filthy lie" by telling his tale. He suggests that the Friar came to know his story because friars and fiends are always good friends.

The Summoner then tells a short story about a friar who dreamt that he went to Hell. When he asked if there were any friars there, Satan lifted his tail and showed him that there were millions of friars swarming around Satan's anus.

THE SUMMONER'S TALE

Summary

There is a district called Holderness in Yorkshire, and a friar who lived there used to urge his parishioners to give more money to friars. To encourage them, he painted a vivid picture of purgatorial torments. After his sermons, he went from house to house begging, and he carried a tablet with him on which to write the names of donors so he could pray for them. He would show the donors that he had written their names down, but as soon as he was out of their homes, he would erase the tablet. (At this point, the Friar interrupts, calling the Summoner a liar, but the Host tells him to continue.)

One day, he called at the home of a man named Thomas. Thomas, who had been ill for several days, asked the friar why he hadn't called on him before. The friar replied that he had been busy praying.

When Thomas' wife entered, the friar embraced her, kissed her and complimented her appearance. He told her that he had come to preach to her husband, and she asked him to scold Thomas because he had been ignoring her in bed. When she asked the friar to stay for dinner, he accepted and requested a number of delicacies, even though he claimed that a friar is supposed to eat very little.

The wife then hinted that his prayers might not be too effective, since her child had died soon after the friar's last visit. The friar wasn't fazed for a moment. He said that he saw in a dream not only the child's death but its entrance into heaven. He then told the wife that friars' prayers were more acceptable to God than anyone else's because friars live in poverty and abstinence.

When Thomas complained that he had already spent most of his money on prayers without receiving any benefit, the friar delivered a long sermon on the dangers of excessive wealth. He told him that instead of scattering his money around, Thomas should give it all to one place — to the friar or his convent.

The friar then delivered a sermon on anger and quoted a number of authorities who see a connection between anger and Satan and vengeful women. He told Thomas that instead of becoming angry, he should give his gold to the convent. When Thomas argued that he had given enough, the friar insisted that he hadn't.

Thomas became very angry at the friar's insistence. Finally, he said he had something he was willing to give. There was one condition — it must be shared equally by all the friars. The friar agreed eagerly, and Thomas told him to reach down underneath his rear end for something he had hidden there for safe-keeping. When the friar did this, Thomas farted loudly.

Furious, the friar left and went to the nearby home of a wealthy man. He told him how he had been insulted. The rich man's wife was amazed that such a thing would happen, but her husband pondered the problem posed by Thomas — how could such a thing be divided? His valet then came up with an answer: one friar would kneel at each spoke of a wheel, and Thomas would be strapped to the hub of the wheel. As the wheel was turned, Thomas would fart, and all the friars would share the odor equally. Everyone but the friar thought this was a most amusing and ingenious answer.

Commentary

No specific source is known for this tale, but stories at the expense of begging friars were common. The nearest analogue to Chaucer's tale is the French *Dis de la Vescie a Prestre* (Story of the Priest's Bladder).

The begging friars were members of the mendicant orders. They were supposed to live in complete poverty and beg only what they needed to live from day to day. By Chaucer's time, many of these orders had grown very wealthy, but their members still continued to beg — not for their daily sustenance, but for profit. The satire in "The Summoner's Tale" derives from the contrast between the ideals of the mendicant orders and the actual behaviour of this friar.

The friar's technique is like the Pardoner's, though not so accomplished. It is not long before the reader sees him as a cheat. After a general description of the friar's methods, the tale focuses upon a specific instance that will illustrate them.

Not only does the friar deceive people, but he also breaks virtually every rule that a friar must follow. Friars were expected to live lives of poverty and abstinence, but the money he collects, the meat he eats, and his flirtations with Thomas' wife suggests that this friar rarely follows these dictates. He also delivers long sermons about gluttony and anger and then displays both of these qualities himself. Furthermore, he continually makes reference to the fact that he is somehow better than other people, because he is a friar and follows such strict rules.

The final irony is, of course, that the friar's theory of behavior towards the different social classes has been proved totally wrong. The lower-class Thomas has outwitted him, and this turning of the tables is made even more amusing by the eagerness with which the friar comes to receive the "gift." He is so greedy that he loses all self-respect.

THE CLERK'S PROLOGUE

Summary

The Host turns to the Clerk and points out that he hasn't spoken since they left. He has been as staid as a newly wedded woman, and the Host suspects that he is thinking about his studies. There is a proper time for everything, however, and now is the time for him to tell the pilgrims a "merry tale." The Host warns him to avoid preaching to them and asks him to make his tale easy for them to understand.

The Clerk gives in to the Host's authority and agrees to tell the pilgrims a tale that he learned from Petrarch, the Italian poet and scholar.

THE CLERK'S TALE

Summary

PART I

In the western part of Italy there is a region called Saluzzo. The marquis of this region was Walter, a young man well-loved and respected by all. He had one fault — he refused to marry. This upset his subjects, and a group of them came to him one day to plead with him to find a wife. After all, he would not always be a young and handsome man, and no one could be sure when death might claim them. They offered to choose a wife for him so that when he died, the royal bloodline would not die with him.

The marquis was moved by their concern and, although he had promised himself that he would never marry, he agreed to find a wife and marry her. He declined their offer of finding a wife for him, saying that he would prefer to choose his own wife.

They were still worried that he would not carry out this plan, so the group asked him to name a date upon which the wedding would take place. After he provided them with a date, they returned to their homes. The marquis then instructed all his knights and his squires to begin the preparations for the wedding celebration.

PART II

Not far from the palace there was a village where a poor

peasant named Janicula lived with his daughter, Griselda. Griselda was not only beautiful, but also virtuous and hard-working. The marquis had often seen her while out hunting and had thought to himself, if I marry, I will marry her.

When the day for the wedding arrived, the marquis' subjects became worried because he had not yet revealed the identity of his bride-to-be. Even so, the marquis ordered his jewelers and tailors to make jewels and gowns for his new wife and made sure the palace was well-prepared for the arrival of Griselda.

Meanwhile, Griselda, not knowing that the marquis had privately selected her as his future wife, spent the morning doing her chores so that she could watch the marriage procession later. As she was carrying some water back to her home, however, she heard the marquis call for her and ask her to bring her father to him. The marquis asked Janicula for permission to marry his daughter and he agreed. The marquis then asked Griselda, who also agreed, though she was shocked by his request. Griselda also swore that she would always obey him, even if it caused her pain, and that she would never complain about any request he made of her.

After the wedding, everyone celebrated long into the night. It wasn't long before people forgot that Griselda had been the daughter of a poor peasant. In the days that passed, she was even more virtuous than before, and everyone loved and honored her. News of her goodness spread beyond the region, and visitors came from many other areas to see her. Her wisdom and understanding helped many of her subjects through troubled times. Soon Griselda gave birth to a baby girl, and, though they would have preferred a boy, her subjects were glad that she was not barren.

PART III

Shortly after this, the marquis felt the need to test his wife's patience and obedience. He told her that his subjects wanted him to take her daughter from her. Griselda remembered her vows and allowed him to send a courier to take the baby away.

When the baby was taken, Griselda did not protest, even though she was certain that her daughter would be murdered by the courier. The marquis was moved by her obedience, but he still ordered that the baby be taken in secret to his sister in Bologna to be cared for. Griselda continued to obey her husband, never mentioning her daughter's name and never revealing that her love for him was any less than when they were married.

PART IV

After four years, Griselda give birth again — this time to a boy. Everyone was relieved that there was now an heir to the throne. When the boy was only two years old, the marquis decided once again to test his wife. He told her that she must now give up her son. Although she was sure her son would be killed, Griselda agreed to let him be taken from her. She told the marquis that she had promised to submit to his will when she married him, and if he were to order her death, she would comply just as willingly. The boy was also taken to Bologna, although Griselda did not know of this.

The marquis marvelled at Griselda's patience and obedience, and even more so at her continuing love for him. Meanwhile, the love his subjects had once felt towards him had turned to hatred. As far as they knew, he had had his children murdered.

When his daughter was twelve years old and his son was ten, the marquis decided to test his wife again. He had a counterfeit papal decree drawn up, declaring him to be free of Griselda and allowing him to marry again. He sent word to his sister that his children were to be returned to him in secret.

PART V

While his children were journeying toward Saluzzo, the marquis called his wife and informed her that his subjects wished him to marry again — this time a woman of nobler birth. The Pope had granted him permission, and his second wife-to-be was on her way. He suggested that Griselda simply return home to live with her father.

Griselda took the news well and said that she realized that her low birth had never been appropriate for the wife of such a great man. She was willing to return to her birthplace, and she wished her husband and his new wife much happiness. She took nothing with her but a smock, and as she walked home to her father in her bare feet, the people who watched her wept.

PART VI

When the marquis' children arrived, he sent for Griselda and asked her to help with the preparations for his wedding. He pretended that his daughter was to be his second wife, and his subjects were pleased and excited that she was so beautiful and refined.

The marquis then called for Griselda and asked her what she thought of his future wife. Griselda, who did not recognize her daughter, praised her beauty but warned the marquis not to test her in the same way as she appeared to be more delicate.

Finally, the marquis was so moved by Griselda's patience that he confessed that his "future wife" and her brother were in fact their children. He told her that his only intention had been to keep them from her "until I had proved the purpose of your heart." Griselda was reunited with her children and dressed again in fine clothes and jewels. That night, all their subjects rejoiced, and the feasting was even greater than that on their wedding day. The marquis and his wife lived happily for many years, and after he died, the marquis was succeeded by his son.

The Clerk concludes his tale by pointing out that all wives need not follow Griselda's example completely. However, she does set a good example of how to be patient in the face of all the adversity that God may bring into our lives, since God tests our wills and our virtues.

Addressing the Wife of Bath, the Clerk then says he will sing a song about his tale. In this song, he warns men not to try the patience of their wives as the marquis did. As for the wives, he advises them to stand up for themselves.

Commentary

"The Clerk's Tale " continues the theme that the Wife of Bath had introduced — sovereignty in marriage. When the Host calls on the Clerk to tell a tale, he says that he will relate a story he learned at Padua from Petrarch. Although he says that Petrarch taught him the story, he immediately afterwards indicates he had learned it from a written version, an inconsistency on Chaucer's part probably explained on the ground that "The Clerk's Tale" is an early work partly revised for *The Canterbury Tales*. Moreover, the Clerk of "The Clerk's Prologue" and the Clerk of the "General Prologue" are not consistently portrayed. The Clerk of "The Clerk's Prologue" is a foreign traveller who apparently has entrance into high literary circles in foreign lands. The Clerk in the "General Prologue" is no such man; he is a poverty-striken scholar who, spending what he can get from his friends on books and learning, has difficulty in making ends meet.

The statement that the Clerk has learned his tale from Petrarch was for a long time taken to mean Chaucer had known the Italian poet in Italy. But we must abandon the idea that the greatest living poet of England was on friendly terms with the greatest living poet of Italy. Most critics feel that Chaucer never met Petrarch.

"The Clerk's Tale," telling of the total surrender of sovereignty by a woman to her husband, is the one poem in all of Chaucer's works that irritates critics. The feeling is that both Griselda and Walter are not realistic. Even the Clerk admits that Griseldas are hard to come by: "It were ful hard to fynde now-a-days/In al a toun Grisildes thre or two."

Yet "The Clerk's Tale," like "The Knight's Tale," is a highly conventional story of philosophical morality, which outlines various Christian themes such as inner purity and Christian resignation. The Clerk informs the pilgrims that Griselda is not a model for women to imitate but a model of how to be patient when God tries us. It is a tale about submission, about the voluntary acceptance of suffering.

In some respects, however, "The Clerk's Tale" is also an answer to the tale told by the Wife of Bath. Where she preached the doctrine of female supremacy, the Clerk relates a tale depicting male supremacy. As he describes Griselda, he paints a portrait of a woman who represents the extreme opposite of the Wife of Bath. While the Wife of Bath would likely have argued with the Clerk about this tale, her opportunity to debate is destroyed when the Clerk tells the pilgrims that his tale is a religious lesson.

To indicate that women more often act as the Wife of Bath does — and by inference that it would be better if they behaved themselves as Griselda does — the Clerk delivers the *Envoy*. This is the Clerk's ultimate victory over the Wife of Bath, since she can hardly argue with his advice that women should act as she does — even if this advice is presented in a somewhat ironic light.

THE MERCHANT'S PROLOGUE

Summary

The Merchant says he knows a great deal about grief and care since he has been married to a cruel shrew for two months. His wife is completely opposite to Griselda, and if he were ever free again, the Merchant would remain a bachelor. The Host begs him to tell them about the art of marriage, and, though the Merchant agrees, he says he will say no more about his personal life.

THE MERCHANT'S TALE

Summary

A prosperous knight named January once lived in Pavia, Lombardy. He had been a bachelor for sixty years, but he suddenly had the urge to marry. He felt that marriage was easy and clean and that it was God's wish that men should marry. He also wanted a son to inherit his wealth.

The Merchant praises marriage and wives, and he quotes a number of authorities on the subject. There are many examples of good wives in history and in the Bible: Abigail, Esther, Eve and Judith. Philosophers such as Cato also have praised marriage.

January decided to call all his friends together and ask their advice. He told them that he wanted to marry quickly and that he wanted to marry only a young woman. One of his brothers, Placebo, agreed with his plans. Justinus, January's other brother, disagreed. He felt that choosing a proper wife was a difficult task and not a thing to be hurried.

January remained convinced that he wanted to marry and so set about finding a wife. He looked at many young women and finally decided upon a maiden named May. Once again, he called his friends together to tell them of his decision and to ask their advice. He wanted to know their opinions on why marriage is called a heaven on earth and how a man could be sure that he had chosen the right wife.

Justinus said that this was nonsense and that January's wife would probably make his life a hell on earth. January ignored Justinus' advice and went ahead with his plans for the marriage.

After the wedding, there was a banquet with plenty of

food, wine and entertainment. January was well pleased, but he was impatient for the festivities to end. Finally, the guests left, the priest blessed the wedding-bed, and January enjoyed his honeymoon night with May.

That same night, Damian, one of January's serving-men, was smitten with love when he saw May at the banquet. He was so heart-sick that he became bed-ridden. He wrote a long letter to May, telling her of his undying love.

A few days later, January heard that Damian was ill and sent May and some women to care for him. While they were there, Damian slipped May the letter he had written. May later wrote a letter to him and gave it to him secretly when she visited his sick-bed.

January was living a good life, enjoying his new wife, until he suddenly lost his sight. He became extremely sad, and, as his blindness continued, he began to be very jealous of May. Certain that she would be unfaithful, he demanded that she never leave his side. May still managed to send letters to Damian, however, and sent him a key to a garden with a high wall that January kept locked for his private pleasures.

One day when January wanted to go into the garden with May, she signalled to Damian and he unlocked the gate and hid in a pear tree. Meanwhile, Pluto, the king of fairy land, and his queen, Proserpina, discussed the situation. Pluto wanted to restore January's eyesight because the deception of women was so upsetting. Proserpina, however, said that she would give May a believable excuse when January's sight returned because men are lecherous.

May then walked with January to the pear tree where Damian was waiting and told her husband that she wanted a pear. She convinced him that she would climb the tree and get one, and she was soon in the tree embracing Damian. At that very moment, Pluto restored January's sight, and he saw his wife and Damian in the tree. He yelled at her in a furious rage.

May told January that struggling with a man up a tree was a sure way to restore a person's sight. However, she also told him that his sight was not yet totally restored. He couldn't see quite right, just as someone waking up from a deep sleep can't see well in bright light. January immediately apologized for his outburst, and, when May climbed down from the tree, he embraced her.

84

Commentary

In "The Merchant's Tale," Chaucer returns to the plot of a young woman's infidelity to her older husband. Though this tale has much in common with the plot of "The Miller's Tale," it clearly relates the story in a different tone. "The Merchant's Tale" has far more bitterness; indeed, one scholar calls it the "most sinister" of *The Canterbury Tales*.

The Merchant himself has been involved in an unhappy marriage, and his bitter disappointment is revealed in the way he tells his tale. The names of the characters give an indication to this attitude: January (an old man), May (a young woman), Justinus (the just man), and Placebo (the flattering man).

The marriage represents a union of lust (January) and greed (May). The Merchant scorns January's desire to be married in the way in which he describes the old man's activities in the years prior to his marriage. However, the young love of Damian and May is also treated with contempt. January may be an aging playboy whose lust for May seems disgusting, but Damian and May are presented even more cynically. Although the Merchant sometimes uses the conventions of courtly love to describe their situation (Damian languishing in bed, for instance), all the young couple is really interested in is a sexual, not a platonic, encounter.

"The Merchant's Tale" certainly has its comic moments, but it is obviously not a pure fabliau. Despite its rather grim undertones, however, it is not a pure tragedy either. Perhaps the best way of describing this cynical yet humorous tale is to call it a black comedy.

EPILOGUE TO THE MERCHANT'S TALE

Summary

"My God," the Host cried when the Merchant finished his tale, "save me from a wife like that!" As far as the Host is concerned, women are cunning when it comes to deceiving men, and this tale has proved it. The Host then reveals that he is married to a shrew who has made his life miserable, but he won't list her faults for fear that someone will tell her that he has spoken against her.

THE SQUIRE'S PROLOGUE

Summary

The Host turns to the Squire and asks him to tell a tale about love. The Squire says that he isn't able to speak on that subject, but he will tell a tale, and he hopes he will be excused if he says anything amiss.

THE SQUIRE'S TALE

Summary

PART I

A noble king named Cambuskan once lived at Tsarev in Tartary. He was well-loved by everyone, being compassionate, just, honorable, benevolent and brave. He and his wife, Elpheta, had two sons; the oldest was Algarsyf and the youngest was Cambalo. Their daughter, Canace, was so beautiful that it was impossible to describe her.

When Cambuskan had ruled for twenty years, he decided to celebrate this anniversary with lavish festivities. At the height of the revelry, an unknown knight appeared. This knight was called Gawain, and he was both handsome and graceful. He told the court that he had been asked by his master, the king of India and Araby, to bring good wishes and gifts to Cambuskan. The first gift was the brass horse that Gawain had ridden there. This horse could fly higher and faster than anything they had ever seen. It was made so that by pushing a magic lever in his ear, the animal would change from a statue into a living horse. The second gift was a mirror that showed the person looking into it who his friends and enemies were and what the future held. The foreign king had also sent a ring that allowed whoever wore it to understand and be able to communicate with any living thing, from birds to bushes. The last gift was a sword, which was able to cut through even the strongest armor. Whoever was wounded by the sword could only be healed when the sword was laid flat upon the wound.

After the knight had finished his speech, the king thanked him for the gifts and asked him to join in the festivities. The brass horse was left in the courtyard, the mirror and the sword were put in a tower for safe-keeping, and the ring was given to Canace.

Many people began wondering about the origins and the magical powers of these gifts. Meanwhile, the knight joined the festivities and was chosen to dance with Canace. After a while, the king went with the knight to inspect the brass horse, and the knight explained how it functioned.

PART II

Eventually, the party ended and people began to leave. Canace woke up very early the next day. With her new ring on, she went for a walk in the palace garden. When she heard the birds singing, she could understand what they were saying. She then came upon a falcon who was crying pitifully and bleeding. When Canace asked the bird what was causing her distress, the falcon replied that a young tercel had courted her and won her heart. After a few years, he left her and fell in love with another bird. Ever since then, the broken-hearted falcon had been wandering aimlessly.

Canace took the falcon home with her and bandaged the wounds that, in her distress, the falcon had inflicted upon herself with her own beak.

The Squire says that he will now tell the stories of the rest of the royal family and the ways in which their lives were affected by the gifts from the foreign king.

Commentary

With "The Squire's Tale," Chaucer drops the theme of the marriage problem and turns to an interlude of pure romance. This is not surprising since the Squire is the Knight's son, and the Knight began *The Canterbury Tales* with a tale of romance. However, some critics argue that "The Squire's Tale" functions as a bridge in the "Marriage Group," since it presents ideals of love and gentility similar to those in "The Franklin's Tale." While its ideals contrast with what is presented in "The Wife of Bath's Tale" and "The Merchant's Tale," "The Squire's Tale" uses the same fairy-tale background of these tales.

The Squire tells a story of adventure and enchantment. It contains, to be sure, the sad history of a deserted lady, but even this is made less real by the metamorphosis of the actors into birds. The tale is a perfect expression of the joy and wonder and simple human feeling which gives enduring charm to the numerous metrical romances of medieval Europe. It is clear that

Chaucer, with all the skepticism and sophistication that have been attributed to him, could enter heartily into the spirit of this literature. He "left half-told the story of Cambuscan bold," probably because he had in mind no plan for continuing it. No definite source has been discovered for the tale, and Chaucer was not much given to inventing plots. For what he did write he likely found suggestions in *The Arabian Nights* and in accounts then current of travels in the East. He may have picked up some of his lore from the oral reports of the traders and sailors with whom he was in frequent contact in the port of London. For it is not to be assumed that everything he used came out of books.

THE WORDS OF THE FRANKLIN TO THE SQUIRE

Summary

The Franklin interrupts "The Squire's Tale" and compliments the Squire on his eloquence. He wishes that his son would display the same kind of discretion that the Squire does. Instead, his son ignores all advice and gambles away all his money.

The Host then interrupts the Franklin and reminds him that everyone must tell at least one tale, if not two, before the end of their contest. "Stop talking with the Squire," the Host says, "and tell your own story." The Franklin agrees to tell a tale and hopes that everyone will enjoy it.

THE FRANKLIN'S PROLOGUE

Summary

In the days of the noble Bretons, many delightful adventure stories were told, and the Franklin says that he will attempt to retell one of them. He hopes the pilgrims will excuse his uncultivated language, since he cannot "color" his words the way that skilled rhetoricians can.

THE FRANKLIN'S TALE

Summary

In Brittany, there once lived a knight named Arveragus. He was deeply in love with a lady named Dorigen and did many brave deeds to win her love.

Dorigen was beautiful and well-bred, and eventually she

recognized his worthiness and agreed to marry him. He promised that he would never abuse his authority as a husband and would always trust her. She, in turn, promised to be a true and humble wife.

After the wedding, he took her to his homeland, and they lived happily in a castle not far from Penmarch. After a few years, Arveragus left for Britain to seek glory and honor at arms. He stayed away two years.

Dorigen was upset when her husband left and spent her days mourning and fasting. Gradually, her grieving began to lessen, especially when she started to receive letters from her husband saying that he was well.

Arveragus' castle was near the coast, and Dorigen made it her habit to walk along the shore and ponder the meaning of existence. She often wished that she could see her husband's ship returning. Other times, she would wonder why God had created such a rocky shoreline since so many men lost their ships and their lives because of it. She grew to hate the rocks and wished they would sink into hell.

Her friends could see that walking along the shore only depressed Dorigen, so they planned a picnic for her on a May morning. One of the people who attended the picnic was Aurelius, a young man who had secretly fallen in love with Dorigen. He had been in love with her for two years, yet he had never dared to reveal his feelings. When he got a chance, he spoke with Dorigen and told her of his deep love for her. Dorigen told him that she had no intention of being unfaithful to her husband, but, just for fun, she promised him her love if he could do this impossible task: clear the shoreline of all its dangerous rocks.

Aurelius went home despondent and prayed to Apollo to send a flood that would raise the water above the reach of the rocks so that he could win Dorigen's love. After this, he fainted, and his brother put him to bed and cared for him.

Meanwhile, Arveragus returned home and was happily reunited with his wife. For two years, however, Aurelius lay in bed, sick and tormented by unrequited love. His brother continued to take care of him and eventually learned the cause of his grief. One day, the brother remembered that as a student, he had secretly studied magic and had seen a book full of magical information. He told his brother of this, and Aurelius finally found a student who had studied magic in depth and who had decoded rare magic books. Aurelius offered him £1,000 if he could clear the coast of rocks. The student agreed, and soon after Aurelius returned home the rocks vanished.

Aurelius then approached Dorigen and reminded her of her promise. Dorigen reacted as if she had been struck by lightning. She had never thought that Aurelius would fulfil her incredible demand. She began weeping and when Arveragus returned home, she told him of her predicament. Arveragus told her that although it grieved him, she must honor her promise since truth is the highest thing in this life.

Dorigen then met with Aurelius and told him that her husband had told her that she must preserve her honor and do as she had promised. Aurelius was shocked by Arveragus' nobility and sacrifice and was filled with pity. He could not bear to touch Dorigen and instead sent her back to her husband.

Dorigen and her husband lived in harmony for many years, but meanwhile Aurelius discovered that he only had enough money for half of what he owed the student of magic. He met with the student, who asked him how his plan had worked. When Aurelius told him that he had not taken his pleasure with Dorigen, the student promptly forgave the debt.

The Franklin concludes his tale by posing the question: "who was the finest gentleman in this story?"

Commentary

The Franklin's story is a *Breton lay*, a short tale of adventure that was customarily recited to a musical accompaniment. The most famous examples of Breton lays are those written by Marie de France in the 12th century, most of which are delicate, sad tales of courtly love.

"The Franklin's Tale" opens with a situation typical of courtly love. The knight serves his lady and performs great deeds to win her; he suffers in silence until he can bear it no longer and then tells her of his distress. Now, however, a wrong note enters: the lovers decide to get married. Courtly love was generally considered something extraneous to — even in opposition to — marriage. The Franklin feels constrained by his middle-class morality to have the lovers legally married, but at the same time he realizes that this development is definitely not in the tradition of courtly love, and that some of his audience who have moved in aristocratic social circles may think it unsuitable. Consequently he goes to great pains to explain the relation between the lovers. The knight promises that even after marriage, he will treat his wife like a mistress, and be obedient to her — except that in public she should act as if he were boss, so as not to embarrass him before his friends. Dorigen, in turn, promises freely to obey him and always to be true to him. This whole arrangement must have sounded rather strange to the Franklin's listeners, and throughout the story he tries to make it seem plausible.

"The Franklin's Tale," then, is superficially in the tradition of courtly love, but actually full of highly inappropriate middle-class sentiments: the lovers are married and live happily ever after, and the rejected suitor worries about how much he has spent on his courtship.

THE PHYSICIAN'S TALE

Summary

Livy recorded the story of a well-bred, rich and honorable knight named Virginius. This knight and his wife had one child, an incredibly beautiful daughter, who was fourteen years old. In addition to her great beauty, she was also patient, kind, humble, chaste and temperate. The Physician warns all parents that they should set themselves as good examples for their children to follow, and they should supervise their children closely.

One morning the daughter and her mother went to town. A judge named Appius saw the girl and decided that she was so beautiful, he must have her. He knew that this would be a difficult task, so he devised a plan and paid Claudius, a criminal, a great deal of money to help him carry it out.

Following the judge's plan, Claudius accused Virginius of having stolen a servant-girl from him many years ago and having passed her off as his daughter. He presented this suit to Appius, and, before Virginius had the chance to defend himself, Appius ruled that this girl must be brought to him and given to Claudius until the case was settled.

When Virginius returned home, he told his daughter that she must die or she would have to accept the shame of having her chastity taken from her. Virginius felt that death was preferable to such shame and so beheaded her with his sword.

The despondent Virginius then went to Appius and presented him with the head of his daughter. When he saw the head, Appius immediately accused Virginius of murder and ordered that he be hanged. But the news of Appius' treachery had spread, and, at that moment, one thousand citizens forced their way into the court. They threw Appius in prison and sentenced Claudius to be hung for his role in the scheme. Virginius asked that Claudius be spared and sent into exile instead, and the citizens reluctantly agreed. The moral of the story is, the Physician says, "forsake your sins before they forsake you."

Commentary

Although Chaucer has the Physician attribute his tale to Livy — who related it in his book of Roman history — many scholars believe that Chaucer's source was Jean de Meun's and Guillaume de Lorris' *Roman de la Rose*, which also retells the tale very briefly. It is possible that Chaucer wrote this tale from information in *Roman de la Rose* but also used some details from Livy's account.

Also of interest is the fact that Chaucer did not likely intend the story to be included in *The Canterbury Tales* when he wrote it. In fact, the lengthy discussion of childbearing suggests to some critics that Chaucer may have had personal reasons for writing this tale.

Unlike a "problematic" piece like "The Merchant's Tale," "The Physician's Tale" is very straightforward. The moral of the story is obvious, and there is no irony or intellectual reflection involved in the telling of the tale.

THE PHYSICIAN-PARDONER LINK

Summary

The Host makes a loud and emotional speech about "The Physician's Tale," attacking the treachery of the judge and bemoaning the fate of the girl. He says that "The Physician's Tale" was so sad and moving, he will need either a mug of beer or a merry tale to cheer him up. He asks the Pardoner to tell a funny story, but the rest of the pilgrims protest and demand that the Pardoner tell a moral tale instead. The Pardoner agrees and says he will think of something decent while he has a drink.

Commentary

This link is important with regard to the relationship between the Host and the rest of pilgrims. Although various pilgrims have influenced the order and content of the tales, up until this point most of the pilgrims have been content with the Host's leadership. Now, however, the "gentlefolk," or more refined pilgrims, protest loudly. After all, the tales were to be of *both* "sentence and solass," and the Host's preference for merry tales has begun to upset the balance of the plan that they had all agreed upon.

THE PARDONER'S PROLOGUE

Summary

The Pardoner says that he uses a particular method of preaching in church. He always speaks loudly, and he always preaches the same sermon: "money is the root of all evil." First, he shows the parishioners all his official documents, then he tells stories about high-ranking religious figures and speaks in Latin. After this, he shows them his religious relics, which are actually phoney. He makes extravagant claims for their ability to cure people and make them prosperous. He makes a great deal of money selling these relics to people who believe what he says about them.

A central part of his technique involves preaching against greed, so that the parishioners will be encouraged to donate money to the Pardoner and his church. The Pardoner admits that he is preaching against a vice that he himself has, yet as guilty as he is, he does cause others to repent. He also admits that he thinks nothing of convincing even the poorest people to give their money to him, since he likes to live well.

It is no secret that he is not a moral man, but he will, nevertheless, tell a moral tale. The tale he will tell is one he often uses when he is trying to encourage people to give money to him.

Commentary

The Prologue is a masterpiece of dramatic self-revelation. In it the Pardoner shamelessly analyses the hypocritical way in which he uses his religious office — to preach, and sell indulgences and relics — for his own gain. Repellent as the Pardoner may be as a person, we cannot fail to be impressed by the shrewdness and wit with which he discusses the preacher's craft in his Prologue. He practices the art of oratory with great skill.

An astute psychologist, the Pardoner knows that while his hearers must be made to feel their guilt (so that they will buy absolution from him), they must not be made to feel too guilty. Therefore, he forbids those who have done "horrible sins" to approach him; he will deal only with those whose errors are mild and presumably of a socially acceptable kind. Finally, the Pardoner is adept at finding just the right level on which to combine both instruction and entertainment. He moralizes through the traditional *exempla*, or stories, that the people enjoyed. One such story is the tale that he will tell the pilgrims.

A large part of the Pardoner's account of his activities is concerned with the various objects he carries about with him to impress his listeners, especially his "relics." Money recurs like a refrain in this prologue. It is never far from the Pardoner's thoughts, and it directs all his actions. He is forthright about this and boasts about how much money he makes. The traditional notion of the cleric's self-imposed poverty is laughable to him.

THE PARDONER'S TALE

Summary
Once in Flanders, three young men sat in an inn all night, swearing, drinking, eating and gambling. The Pardoner pauses here to preach against these sins. He suggests that over-eating and drinking were responsible for Lot sleeping with his daughter, Herod killing John the Baptist, and Adam eating the forbidden apple. If people only knew more about what gluttony and drinking leads to, they would be less likely to indulge in either. He notes that St. Paul spoke against gluttony, and the Pardoner attacks cooks who encourage people to overeat. Drunkenness is just as bad, and drunkards are usually foul people. The Bible commands abstinence, and historical examples back up its claims. Gambling leads to lying, cursing and a waste of time and money, and swearing is a sin against God.

The Pardoner returns to his tale about the three wild young men. While they were drinking, they heard a bell ringing, which meant that a coffin was passing by. When they asked who was in the coffin, a serving-boy said that the dead man had been a friend of the three drinkers years ago and that suddenly last night while he was drunk, he was killed by a thief named Death. Death had also killed many other people in the neighborhood.

Even though the people in the town tried to convince the drunken young men of how dangerous Death was, the men decided to track him down and kill him. Shortly after setting off, they vowed to protect one another's lives with their own.

While on their way to the village, they came upon an old man who asked them to be more quiet. They jeered at him and asked him why he hadn't died yet. The old man told them that he had searched all over the world for someone who was willing to exchange their youth for his age, but he couldn't find anyone. Even Death wasn't willing to take the old man's life. He also warned the young men to treat older people with more respect.

One of the young men accused the old man of being Death's spy. The old man then told them that they could find Death waiting under an oak tree up the road, and the young men ran to the tree. When they got there, they found a huge pile of gold. They wanted to take the gold for themselves, but they were afraid of carrying it away in the daytime since people would accuse them of being thieves. They decided to wait until nightfall and to draw lots now to see which one of them would go into the village and get them some food and drink.

They drew lots, and the youngest lost and went off to town. As soon as he left, the two other men plotted to kill him and divide his portion of the gold between them. Meanwhile, the youngest man plotted to kill the two other men and keep the gold for himself. He decided to buy some rat poison, and he poisoned two of the bottles of wine he bought.

When the youngest man returned, the other two men killed him. Afterwards, however, they drank the wine he had bought and so killed themselves as well.

The Pardoner now preaches against the sins of excess, murder, gluttony, gambling and cursing. He reminds the pilgrims that if they have sinned, they can buy his holy pardons and be freed from their wrongdoings. When they buy these pardons from him, he will enter their names in his ledger and will absolve them of their sins. He also reminds them that he has relics for sale. He suggests that the Host might be interested in one of his pardons, since he is obviously the most sinful.

The Host refuses furiously and attacks the Pardoner for being so deceitful. The Pardoner is so angry, he can't speak, and the Knight, seeing that things are getting out of hand, urges the two men to make up.

Commentary

No specific source is known for this tale. However, the basic plot is a very old one, and a similar story has been found in ancient Hindu writings. A version similar to Chaucer's appears in the post-Chaucerian *Cento Novelle Antiche* (A Hundred Old Stories).

The story is designed to indicate the evil of greed, yet the Pardoner has admitted being the most greedy of men. The tale begins with a diatribe against gluttony, sex and especially drunkenness; yet the Pardoner insisted on having a drink before he started to tell it.

The tale consists of three sections and is followed by an epilogue. The first section presents the introductory sermon. The second section contains the story itself. The third section contains the concluding sermon and ends with an attempt to sell some relics.

Just as we expect the narrative to begin, the Pardoner begins a lengthy denunciation of the sins of gluttony, gambling and blasphemy. He does this through a series of illustrative anecdotes, called *exempla*, of which medieval audiences seem to have been particularly fond. Collections of *exempla*, the stories classified according to subject, were prepared for the use of preachers. Some contemporary accounts indicate that sermons were liable to degenerate into nothing more than a string of *exempla*. However, as the Pardoner himself remarks, "lewed peple loven tales olde," and the *exempla* were valuable in giving vivid and memorable form to moral lessons.

After the attack on vices and the retailing of *exempla*, the tale proper finally begins. The style becomes more direct and concentrated, and less rhetorical. Much of the narrative is given in the dialogue of the actors — the three men, the innkeeper, the boy and the old man. This provides a contrast to what has gone before and also gives the immediacy of drama.

The old man the three meet on their way is a figure of significance. From the Middle Ages to the 18th century the figure of an old man has been associated with wisdom and moral rectitude. The insolence with which the three treat the old man would be immediately interpreted by the 14th century person as evidence of moral delinquency. The old man also seeks Death, but not in order to defeat him. Death, as part of God's purpose, is a preliminary to another world, to be welcomed when it comes. Unlike the three men, the old man understands Death. He is in accordance with, rather than in defiance of, God's plan; but the old man is more than simply a character in a drama. He carries a symbolic significance; he is Death himself in disguise.

The three men follow the old man's directions, but instead of the figure of Death they have been told to expect, they find a treasure. They rejoice at this but it is, of course, the story's final irony. The old man is right: given the characters of the three, the gold they find produces the greed that leads to their death. And so the story arrives at the point at which the sermon began: *radix malorum est cupiditas* (love of money is the root of all evil).

THE SECOND NUN'S PROLOGUE

Summary

Idleness is a fiend that encourages vice, and it is always trying to trap us. In fact, the Second Nun decides that she will not risk being idle too long and will instead begin her tale of the life of Saint Cecilia.

She begins with an Invocation to the Virgin Mary in which she asks for assistance in telling her tale accurately. Her story will deal with Cecilia, who managed to conquer the Devil and remain true to her faith. After praising the glories and the goodness of the Virgin Mary, the Second Nun asks for forgiveness for her lack of talent in telling the story of a saint.

Her interpretation of the name Cecilia contains five meanings. Cecilia means: (a) a "lily of heaven," signifying chasteness; (b) "path to the blind," signifying the way she teaches; (c) "heaven's glory," signifying her thoughts of holiness and her unending labor; (d) "wanting in blindness," signifying that she could see the light of the truth; and (e) "a heaven for people," signifying that people can see in her the excellence of her devotion to God.

Commentary

In Chaucer's time, part of a nun's training included instruction in stories of the saints. It is therefore appropriate for the Second Nun to have selected the story of Saint Cecilia for her tale.

As the Prioress did in her prologue, the Second Nun begins by presenting an Invocation to the Virgin Mary. Since her story is concerned with chastity, this is also particularly appropriate.

THE SECOND NUN'S TALE

Summary

There was once a young noblewoman of Rome named Cecilia. She was raised as a Christian and loved chastity so much that she desired never to lose her virginity. On the day she was to be married to a young man named Valerian, she prayed that she might be allowed to remain chaste. After the wedding, she told Valerian that she had a guardian angel who would kill anyone who tried to take away her virginity.

Valerian said that if he could see this angel, he would not touch her, but if she was only saying this because she was in love with another man, he would kill them both. Cecilia said that he must be baptized by Saint Urban before he could see the angel.

When Valerian found Saint Urban, the saint was overjoyed to see that Cecilia had convinced her husband to be baptized. A vision appeared before them of an old man who said there is only one God and one faith. When the vision disappeared, Valerian was baptized.

Valerian returned home and found Cecilia standing with an angel in their room. The angel gave a crown of lilies to Cecilia and a crown of roses to Valerian. The flowers were from Paradise, and they would never die or lose their fragrance. Also, no one could see them unless they were chaste.

Valerian told the angel that he had a brother that he loved more than anyone else and that he would like him to know the truth about God. Meanwhile, Tiburce, his brother, arrived and was overwhelmed by the flowers from Paradise. Valerian told him what had happened and urged him to be baptized. But Tiburce was reluctant to lead the life of a man like Saint Urban, who was hunted and jeered at by non-Christians. Cecilia explained that their life on earth meant nothing since Christ has told them of an afterlife. Tiburce then asked her other questions about the Christian faith, and Cecilia explained them to him. Tiburce was then baptized and became a Christian, too.

Eventually, the two brothers were arrested by Roman officers and brought to Almachius. He questioned them and ordered that they make a sacrifice to the pagan gods of Rome. They refused and were executed. Before they died, however, they told their story to Maximus, one of the Roman officers, and he was also converted to Christianity. When Maximus saw the souls of the two brothers rise to Heaven, he converted many others. After a while, he, too, was executed.

Cecilia was then brought before Almachius and questioned. She defied his orders and boldly mocked his questions. Almachius became furious and ordered that she be killed by being placed in boiling water, but Cecilia suffered no pain when they put her in the water. He then tried to have her killed by having her head cut off with a sword, but this was also unsuccessful. Although she was badly cut, Cecilia lived for three more days and continued to preach Christianity until the end. When she finally died, she asked that her house be made into a church. Saint Urban buried her in secret in the graveyard of the saints, and her house came to be known as the Church of Saint Cecilia.

Commentary

Legends of the lives of the saints were popular in Chaucer's age. Like "The Physician's Tale," this story was probably not written for *The Canterbury Tales*. Indeed, when the Second Nun refers to herself as the "unworthy son of Eve," it is clear that even as a part of *The Canterbury Tales*, this tale was not designed for a female speaker. Chaucer's source was almost definitely Jacobus Voragine's *Legenda Aurea*, since his story matches the account in this book very closely.

Like "The Prioress' Tale," this tale is entirely focused upon religion. It reflects the popular trend in religious stories of the time — miracles and martyrdom.

THE CANON'S YEOMAN'S PROLOGUE

Summary

Shortly after the Second Nun had finished her tale, two men rode up to speak with the pilgrims. One was a Canon, or so the pilgrims guessed from his clothes, and the other was his Yeoman. Both men had been riding their horses hard, and the Canon said that they had been trying to catch up with the pilgrims for some time. They were both courteous and eager to join the pilgrims on their journey.

The Host welcomes them and asks eagerly if the Canon has a joke to tell them. The Yeoman tells the Host that his master is a great teller of jokes. When the Host inquires about his occupation, the Yeoman says that his master is an alchemist. He is a wise man, the Yeoman says, but he will never been successful. They live in the kinds of places thieves live in because they are afraid of being discovered at their craft. The Yeoman says his face is discolored because of the fires they use in alchemy.

The Canon suddenly tells his Yeoman to stop talking about their work, but the Host interrupts and tells the Yeoman to continue. When the Canon realizes that all his secrets are about to be revealed, he rides away. The Yeoman is glad that he has left since their business has never been anything but misery and long hours with no success. Now that his master is gone, he will try to tell their story to the pilgrims.

Commentary

The arrival of the Canon and his Yeoman provides an interesting diversion for both the pilgrims and the reader. Even though neither man has been riding with the pilgrims and neither is officially part of the contest, the Host asks them to tell a tale anyway.

The Canon's reaction to his Yeoman's revelation that they are alchemists reflects the secrecy with which alchemy was carried out. The church disapproved of alchemy, and most alchemists in the Middle Ages worked in extreme isolation. The constant failures the Yeoman refers to also reflect a reality of the time since there is no historical record of a successful alchemical transformation of a base metal into gold.

THE CANON'S YEOMAN'S TALE

Summary
PART I

The Canon's Yeoman has worked for the Canon for more than seven years, and he is no closer to being able to produce gold than he was when he started. He is also deeply in debt, and his skin and eyes have been damaged from his work. The Canon and his Yeoman have tried many different mixtures in their attempts to produce gold, but all of their experiments have failed.

The Yeoman then describes in detail some of the chemicals and methods they have used, and he tells the pilgrims that any of them who are interested in alchemy would be wasting their time and money since they would also fail to create gold. No one can discover the secret of the Philosopher's Stone (the secret of making gold). He warns them that all they will get for their efforts is poverty and a bad smell. Alchemists may think they are very wise, but they are actually the biggest fools of all.

PART II

There was once a priest who had lived for many years in London. A canon (not the Yeoman's master) borrowed a mark from him and promised that he would repay it in three days. Sure enough, the canon returned in that time with the mark that he owed the priest, and the priest was delighted at his promptness. To show his appreciation, the canon also offered to reveal some alchemical secrets. He asked the priest to get him some quicksilver and coal. He sent the priest's servant out of the room and got the fire going so that he could heat his mixtures. By trickery, he convinced the priest that he had turned the quicksilver into silver by adding some mysterious powder to it. The priest was amazed. The canon then pretended to put an ingot of chalk in the fire, but when the priest wasn't looking, he replaced it with an ingot of silver. Finally, the canon had a charred piece of wood in which a hole had been bored. It was filled with silver filings, and the hole was plugged with wax. After he put this into the fire, the wax melted and the silver poured out. The canon then put an ounce of copper in the fire and when the priest wasn't looking, he replaced the molten copper with silver. The priest was deceived a fourth time and thought that the canon and his alchemical secrets really could produce silver.

The priest urged the canon to have the silver he believed the canon had created tested. The silversmith said that it was genuine, and the priest was overjoyed. He asked to buy some of the canon's "magic powder," and the canon agreed to sell it to him for £40 on the condition that he would not reveal these alchemical secrets. The canon then left town quickly, and the priest never saw him again.

The Canon's Yeoman then delivers a short speech on alchemists. He ridicules their jargon and their constant failures. He feels that God will not allow man to discover the secret of creating precious metals, and man should not, therefore, go contrary to God's will.

Commentary

The first part of this tale is actually an extension of its prologue. Both recall the dynamic qualities of the Wife of Bath and the Pardoner.

"The Canon's Yeoman's Tale" is essentially a lengthy argument against alchemy — a quasi-science based on the belief that it is possible to turn base metals into precious metals, usually gold, through the manipulation of heat and the addition of a number of chemicals and other ingredients. His argument begins with a monologue full of interjections and asides. In Part II, the Yeoman becomes less conspicuous as a narrator, and his tale follows the convention of a philosophical amplification of his own experiences and beliefs.

THE MANCIPLE'S PROLOGUE

Summary

The pilgrims are getting closer to Canterbury, and suddenly the Host notices that the Cook is almost falling off his horse. The Cook is drunk, and the Host tries to rouse him from his stupor. He is unsuccessful, and the Manciple offers to tell a tale in the meantime.

He criticizes the Cook for being so drunk, and the Cook finally falls off his horse. After they get him back in his saddle, the Host tells the Manciple not to be so critical. The Manciple apologizes and gives the Cook some wine to drink. The Host notes how easily harmony is restored when alcohol is offered.

THE MANCIPLE'S TALE

Summary

There was once a handsome young man named Phoebus. He was a skilled warrior, and a good musician and singer. He was also renowned for his generosity and courage. For his amusement, Phoebus kept a white-feathered crow in a cage and taught it how to mimic speech.

Pheobus had a wife he loved very much, and he was always trying to please her. He was, however, a very jealous man, and he tried to keep his wife from other people.

Any animal or bird will long for freedom if it is locked up, and while Phoebus was out of town, his wife sent for her secret lover, and they spent the night together.

The talking crow told Phoebus what had happened when he returned home, and Phoebus killed his wife in a jealous rage. Shortly after, he was overcome with grief and remorse, and he took his revenge upon the bird. He plucked out its beautiful white feathers and replaced them with black ones. He also took away its ability to sing and talk.

The Manciple then states that the moral of the story is that you should never tell a man of his wife's infidelity, because he will hate you for it. You should learn instead to "hold your tongue" and restrain yourself from saying something before you have thought it through.

Commentary

Chaucer's source for this tale was Ovid's *Metamorphoses,* but the story of the "tell-tale bird" is a very common folktale. The tale is a straightforward one, and its moral is clear. It is interesting, however, that the message of the story concerns gossip and not either jealousy or adultery.

THE PARSON'S PROLOGUE

Summary

By the time "The Manciple's Tale" is over, it is late in the afternoon. The Host turns to the pilgrims and says that there is only one story left to be told. He asks the Parson to tell the last tale.

The Parson says that he will not tell any fables or romances, since St. Paul said that they distort the truth. Instead, he will give them something that contains moral teaching. He warns them that he is not a good speaker and that he is not very learned. The Host asks him to begin his sermon but warns him to be quick because night will soon fall.

Commentary

It is interesting that the Parson — one of the most virtuous men on the pilgrimage — should find fables and romances so offensive since so many of the tales he has heard have been of this nature. He rejects tales of "solass" and wants to tell instead a tale of "sentence."

Also of note is the fact that the Host says all of the tales that they had planned for have been told. Obviously, this section was written when Chaucer still anticipated the completion of *The Canterbury Tales*.

THE PARSON'S TALE

Summary

God does not want anyone to perish, and He has outlined many different ways to the celestial city (salvation). One way is penitence, which means that we are sorry for our sins and have the will not to sin again. Contrition is the heart's sorrow for sin.

There are two kinds of sin: venial and deadly. Venial sin is loving Christ less than we should. Deadly sin is loving another person more than God. Venial sin may lead to deadly sin.

There are seven deadly sins, and the first one is *pride*. Pride is displayed in arrogance, boasting or hypocrisy. Pride may be inward or outward. The cure for pride is true self-knowledge or humility.

We show *envy* when we are unhappy with the prosperity of others and glad when they are hurt. It is the worst sin. The cure for envy is to love God, your neighbor and your enemy.

Anger is the next deadly sin. It is expressed in vengeance, but anger directed against evil is good. Anger leads to hatred, murder, treachery, lies, scorn and curses. The cure for anger is patience.

Sloth is the sin committed when we do things with irritation, poorly and without joy. Sloth leads to despair. Its cure is fortitude.

Avarice is a sin that expresses itself in a lecherous desire for earthly sins. It leads to fraud, gambling, theft and sacrilege. Its cure is mercy.

Gluttony is an enormous appetite for food or drink. The cure for gluttony is abstinence.

Lechery is like gluttony. It destroys the body and soul. Its cure is chastity.

When we make confession, we must make it with free will and in full faith. It must not be a hasty act but a carefully considered act. It should be frequent. Satisfaction can be achieved by giving to the poor and by practising penance, fasting and bodily pains. Its reward is eternal bliss in heaven.

Commentary

Although the Parson says that he will "tell a merry tale in prose," what follows is, of course, a sermon. It is, however, totally appropriate for the Parson to preach at this point. He is a religious man, and he has patiently waited his turn while several other pilgrims have told bawdy stories and have acted in a manner that would be offensive to him (the Cook's drunkenness, for example). It seems fitting that the Parson should preach about the seven deadly sins after we have experienced all of them in either the tales or the behavior of the pilgrims. With both "The Parson's Tale" and its prologue, we are reminded that the journey to Canterbury is not merely a social event but a spiritual one.

CHAUCER'S RETRACTION

Summary

Chaucer includes a series of retractions at the end of *The Canterbury Tales*. If the reader discovers some tales that please him, he should thank Christ. If the reader discovers tales that displease him, Chaucer apologizes and says that he wrote the tales as well as he could and his only intention was to serve God.

He asks God to forgive him for his sins — especially for a number of his writings and translations, including the tales in *The Canterbury Tales* that "tend toward sin."

He thanks Christ and the Virgin Mary for his religious writing and asks that he may be granted the grace of "true penance, confession and satisfaction."

Commentary

The placement of the retractions within the structure of *The Canterbury Tales* supports its implicit connection with the Parson's prologue and tale. Following the advice given in "The

Parson's Tale,'' Chaucer confesses his sins and seeks forgiveness and reconciliation with God through repentance. However, the reader is left with the problem of accepting for himself a rejection of the "bawdy" tales.

If we consider the "frame" of *The Canterbury Tales* as a tale in itself, then we can see it as a tale of Chaucer the pilgrim. It tells the story of Chaucer the pilgrim's journey from ignorance to knowledge. Repentance is based on a knowledge of vices, and the journey through the tales — both those of "solass" and those of "sentence" — is, therefore, a necessary one.

The Principal Characters

The principal characters of *The Canterbury Tales* include the group of pilgrims who met at the Tabard Inn and decided to journey together to a shrine in Canterbury, two other men (the Canon and his Yeoman) who join them along the way and the Host who decides to accompany them and supervise the tale-telling contest. These characters represent many aspects of medieval life since they came from many different social classes and occupations. However, they also represent many different kinds of people, and this is what makes these characters so timeless in their appeal.

The Knight: An honorable warrior who fought for Christianity against heathens.

The Squire: The Knight's son; a lusty youth and an accomplished soldier.

The Yeoman: A servant to the Knight and the Squire and an expert hunter.

The Prioress: A worldly superior of a nunnery, accompanied by another nun and three priests.

The Second Nun: She accompanies the Prioress as a kind of personal secretary.

The Nun's Priest: One of the priests who accompanies the Prioress and the only one who tells a tale.

The Monk: A fat, bald lover of hunting and luxury who rejects work or study.

The Friar: A merry man who is an accomplished beggar for his own gain.

The Merchant: A pompous businessman who talks honestly while actually practising illegal moneylending.

The Clerk: A threadbare student who prefers philosophy and books to riches.

The Man of Law: One of a select group of lawyers; equal to the Knight in social standing.

The Franklin: A wealthy landowner and civic leader who is fond of good food.

The Haberdasher, Carpenter, Weaver, Dyer and Carpet Maker: They are wealthy tradesmen and members of the same parish guild.

The Cook: The private cook for the members of the guild.

The Shipman: An accomplished sailor and drinker.

The Physician: A learned doctor with a love for money.

The Wife of Bath: A lusty widow who has enjoyed many pilgrimages and five marriages.

The Parson: A poor, diligent cleric who aids parishioners with his own money.

The Plowman: Brother of the Parson; a hard-working, honest man and a devoted Christian.

The Miller: A wealthy, large and brawny tradesman; talkative and bawdy.

The Manciple: A shrewd kitchen supervisor for a law school.

The Reeve: The crafty manager of a lord's property.

The Summoner: A lecherous cleric who permits his parishioners to sin for a price.

The Pardoner: The Summoner's companion who sells fake holy relics and pardons from Rome.

The Canon's Yeoman: An alchemist's assistant, he quits his job and joins the pilgrimage.

Chaucer: The narrator who accompanies the pilgrims and recounts the tales and the pilgrim's conversations.

The Host: The commanding, genial innkeeper who proposes the tale-telling contest and supervises it during the pilgrimage.

Critical Analysis

The Development of Medieval Poetry: Themes and Forms

Old English literature — and Germanic literature generally — form a body of work that is heroic and dignified in nature. With the introduction of Christianity into England, Christ and the Virgin Mary replaced Norse gods such as Thor and Odin as subjects, but the literature still remained highly serious.

Old English poetry was composed aloud, before an audience, according to accepted formulas. The poet was not expected to display originality in themes and subject matter, but rather to combine ingeniously the traditional formulas. He accompanied himself with a harp. The poet, or *scop* ("one who shapes"), had the place of honor nearest the chief in front of the fire.

The poetic system underwent a change with the Norman Conquest in 1066. The English language and literature were cut off from the Germanic areas of the continent. The ruling classes in England spoke French and were interested in French literature, particularly the romance. The literature that developed in England during this period combined the Germanic and the French backgrounds.

Religious subjects were very popular. People of the Middle Ages viewed life as a brief pilgrimage on earth. Man should regard this brief period of life primarily as an opportunity to prepare for the world after death. No matter how well man thinks he has prepared himself for the afterlife, the ways of God remain inscrutable. Man cannot presume to understand God's justice — he can only submit.

The medieval man believed that virtue consists in action. Even the worst sinner is better than the person who has drifted through life without ever having done anything worthy of either praise or blame.

The people of the Middle Ages also believed that God would punish an entire nation for the sins of one man. Therefore, they considered it essential for the protection of everyone to stamp out sin everywhere.

The Tradition of Courtly Love

Chaucer often alludes to an attitude or lifestyle called

courtly love. This medieval conception is presented in both his tales of romance and in his fabliaux, or "merry" tales. In the romances, Chaucer presents courtly love as an ideal to be aspired toward; elsewhere, courtly love is often parodied or mocked. A history of courtly love provides us with an idea of how this tradition influenced the lives and literature of the Middle Ages.

Around the end of the 11th century and the beginning of the 12th, poets began for the first time to concentrate on a new subject: love between man and woman. This development appeared first in Provence and spread to the rest of Europe. It was introduced into England by Henry II's queen, Eleanor of Aquitaine — one of the most intelligent and fascinating women in history.

When the Germans first invaded the Roman Empire, they were nomadic; they had no feeling for land, only for the *comitatus*, the band of fighting men who followed their chief in warring and plundering. Eventually, however, the Huns pushed the Germanic tribes as far as the ocean, and they could no longer go wherever they wanted but were forced to settle down. Now land acquired great value, since the supply of it was limited. Each chief tried to consolidate his possession of as much land as he could. However, if after a chief's death his land was divided equally among his children, and subsequently among *their* children, inevitably the amount each one possessed would eventually be small. Consequently the people of the early Middle Ages had to devise some system whereby estates would not be constantly divided and subdivided.

The *Salic Law* of the Franks stipulated that women could not inherit property. To solve the problem of too many male heirs, the system of *primogeniture* developed, whereby the oldest son inherited the entire estate and the younger ones were left to shift for themselves. They might enter the church, or if there were a Crusade going on, they might become Crusaders. Crusaders were especially useful in solving the problem of surplus younger sons. If they were not killed, they might manage to carve out a fief for themselves in the Holy Land. However, if there were no Crusades going on, a younger son who did not want to enter the church had to become a knight in the service of some powerful lord. Unless he could somehow acquire a fief, he would have no land to pass on to his children, and they would be commoners. Hence these landless knights could not afford to marry unless they could marry an heiress — which was unlikely.

The population of gentlefolk in a representative castle, then, might consist of a duke and duchess, their eldest son and his wife, their eldest daughter and her husband, a few younger daughters and ladies-in-waiting (who, if they could not make suitable marriages, would eventually be sent off to a nunnery), and perhaps several hundred knights-at-arms, who were young and full of vigor but who could not afford to marry and have legitimate children. Most of the noble ladies had married purely for reasons of convenience, and it was taken for granted that they would have lovers; but with so many knights to choose from, they faced a problem of selection. The conventions of courtly love provided a means of testing suitors; only the bravest, most devoted and most accomplished could hope to pass the test.

The lover was expected to court his lady humbly and devotedly for at least two years before receiving his reward. He should be an accomplished poet, dancer and musician. He was also expected to display conspicuous bravery. The courtly lover, was in all aspects, meant to be an ideal man.

The Fabliau

Many of the most popular stories in *The Canterbury Tales* are fabliaux. A discussion of this form of fiction will help to clarify both the intentions and the historical background of these tales of "solass" that have proved to be the most timeless of all Chaucer's works.

The fabliau originated in medieval France; most of the surviving ones date from the 13th and 14th centuries. Fabliaux are short stories in verse, addressed to a middle-class audience, and their subject matter is usually either bawdy or obscene. The two principal collections of fabliaux are those of Montaiglon and Bédier (both in French). R. H. Robbins has translated into English 100 short stories of the 15th century in a volume called *The Hundred Tales*. These are not true fabliaux, but they are very close.

As far as we know, there were only two fabliaux written in English before Chaucer, *Dame Siriz* and *Reynard the Fox*. In *Dame Siriz*, a young clerk has fallen in love with Lady Margery, and, when the lady's husband is out of town on business, he makes advances to her, which she indignantly refuses. The despondent clerk then goes to an old witch, Dame Siriz, and tells him her troubles. Dame Siriz promises him that for a fee she will guarantee to make the lady more accommodating. After the clerk has paid her some money, she gives her little dog mustard seeds to make it cry. When the dog is weeping satisfactorily, Dame Siriz takes it around to Lady Margery's house. When the lady sees the old woman with the sorrowful dog, she invites them in and asks what has made the animal so unhappy. Dame Siriz replies that the dog is actually her daughter, who has just this morning been magically turned into this form by a young clerk whose advances she had rejected; she is crying over her metamorphosis. Lady Margery, horrified, tells Dame Siriz about her own experience with the clerk, and asks whether a similar fate might befall her. The old woman remarks that clerks are a dangerous lot, full of magical lore; but for a fee she will undertake to find this clerk and bring him to Lady Margery so that the lady will have a chance to treat him more kindly. When Lady Margery has paid her, Dame Siriz goes to the clerk and tells him that the lady will now become his mistress. Sure enough, when the clerk returns to the lady, he finds her perfectly amenable. (She does not tell him the real reason for her change of heart, but says she repented because she feared he might kill himself in his despair.)

In the fabliau of *Reynard the Fox*, the clever fox succeeds in cuckolding the wolf and then having the wolf apologize to *him*.

After Chaucer, a few other English authors began to write fabliaux. One of the last to be written appears in Stephen Hawes' *Pastime of Pleasure* (1509).

Selected Criticism

There is no harm in being reminded that when Chaucer appears in any of his poems he is just as much a creation of the poet as the eagle or the Prioress or the Cook. If, as Manly tried to show, he based his description of some of the pilgrims on actual people whom he had known or observed in real life, he was doing only what poets and novelists and dramatists have always done. But whereas we cannot be certain that Thomas Pynchbek was the prototype of the Man of Law, there can be no doubt about the identity of the narrator who joined the "wel nine and twenty" other pilgrims at the Tabard Inn. And just as we need not suppose that the Man of Law corresponds in all respects with the real Sergeant of the Law whom Chaucer was thinking of, so we need not believe that every characteristic attributed to the pilgrim-narrator, or the "I" of other poems, is a faithful reflection of the poet himself. In most descriptions some features are heightened, some suppressed. Chaucer may, for reasons of discretion, have portrayed some of the pilgrims in *The Canterbury Tales* as recognizable without being legally identifiable. For other reasons he may have represented himself as slow-witted, inexpert in love, or slightly ridiculous.

Albert C. Baugh, "Chaucer the Man," Companion to Chaucer Studies

Chaucer had an immense enthusiasm for life in this world; for the society of his fellow-creatures, high and low, good and bad; for real men and women — knights and sumners, millers and parsons, monks and merchants, delicate cloistered ladies and boisterous wives of Bath. Whatever was good of its kind was a delight to him. And he had such stupendous luck in always meeting nonpareils! There was no better priest than the Parson anywhere; no such Pardoner from one end of England to the other; never so great a purchaser as the Man of Law. If you sought from Hull to Carthage, you couldn't find a mariner to match the Shipman. The Wife of Bath was so excellent a cloth-maker that she actually beat the Dutch. The Sumner's bass voice was more than twice as loud as a trumpet. The Friar was the best beggar in his convent. Why, when the rascally alchemist came riding post-haste to join the Pilgrims, whom he hoped to interest in some of his confidence games, he was perspiring so admirably that Chaucer gazed at him with rapture.

"It was joye for to seen him swete!" cries the poet in high delight. A joy indeed, — he did it in such a thoroughly competent way!

George Kittredge, *Chaucer and his Poetry*

The "frame" of *The Canterbury Tales*, the pilgrimage, and the dialogue of the narrators, has rightly been much admired. We see a wide range of representative temperaments and traditions, intellectual, social, sexual; and because we see them in individuals talking and behaving, values define each other in the way social groups, as well as plays, do define values. The pilgrimage is Chaucer's final step into drama, his last exploration of his world, whose elements define each other and whose connections form a whole. If so *The Canterbury Tales* are more Chaucer's criticism of life than the Moral Ballades. In all senses *The Canterbury Tales* are a journey in Chaucer's company across fourteenth-century England.

Ian Robinson, *Chaucer and the English Tradition*

The freedom he gave his pilgrims, including the Host, was parallel to the freedom he felt he had himself. They could quarrel, argue, seek to impose themselves and their visions, or hide behind a facade of respectability; they could admire, love, reflect their piety in their actions and utterances; they could reveal their virtues and vices and be themselves. He would report them as they were, whatever they said or did, enjoying to the full the variety and the plenitude, secure in the knowledge that if he were true enough to the Great Creation in his own, the pattern and the meaning would emerge.

Charles A. Owen, "The Design of the Canterbury Tales," *Companion to Chaucer Studies*

To describe *The General Prologue to the Canterbury Tales* as the greatest portrait gallery in English literature — if not in all literature — is a cliché of literary history, sufficiently accurate as a reminder that it is largely composed of a series of sketches differing widely in length and in method and blending the individual and the typical in varying degrees. Like all clichés, however, terms such as "portrait gallery" and "historical record" are both vague and inaccurate as applied to the *Prologue*, for it is much more than a collection of character sketches: it reveals the author's intention in bringing together a heterogeneous assortment of people and narrative materials, sets the tone for the storytelling, makes clear the plan for the *Tales*, helps to motivate the telling of several of them, and acquaints the reader with some of the author's attitudes toward both literature and life.

Thomas A. Kirby, "The General Prologue," *A Companion to Chaucer Studies*

The two sides of Chaucer the man — public servant and poet — emerge quite clearly from the accumulated scholarship of the last two centuries. That the picture has undergone changes was to have been expected. One thing is obvious. Chaucer, like Shakespeare later, was a busy man of affairs. The positions he filled and the missions on which he was sent were laborious ones. It must often have been very difficult for him to find the time for reading, which he so much loved — "On bokes for to rede I me delyte" (*Prol LGW*, 30) — and still more the quiet necessary for writing. Much of his poetry must have been written in such intervals as he was able to salvage from a busy, active life. That he had the urge to write goes without saying. That his story-telling gifts were appreciated can hardly be doubted, and may have reinforced the urge, for it is natural to want to do what one knows one does well. That his success was due in an important measure to the personality that shines through every page of his poetry is altogether likely. It is this personality that marks him off from most other Middle English poets, indeed from most other English poets of any age.

Albert C. Baugh, "Chaucer the Man," *Companion to Chaucer Studies*

The continuing delight we feel in the poetry of Chaucer is the sign that we should continue to think about him. So long as there is something wonderful about Chaucer's poetry, the English language will continue to be a language of great poetry of which Chaucer is the father.

Ian Robinson, *Chaucer and the English Tradition*

Chaucer's world was complex. London, the focal point, was a place of paradox: it resounded with the construction of churches and palaces proclaiming the glory of God and of man; it was the arena for ruthless political maneuvers, bitter trade dissensions and wide-scale suffering caused by inhumanity, poverty and disease. If it was, as Dunbar considered it a century later, "the flower of cities," it must also have been the place where "the smylere with the knyf under the cloke" was as real as the sow that "freten the child right in the cradel." A knowledge of the background enables us to set Chaucer's work in its perspective and, in particular, to appreciate its *Weltanschauung*. In a troubled world, Chaucer's poetic vision and artistic sense remain secure; he contemplates the diversity in life with serenity and understanding, and translates it into art by a genius which we cannot explain.

Clair Olson, "Chaucer and Fourteenth-Century Society,"
Companion to Chaucer Studies

Suggested Study Topics

1. What is the relationship between Chaucer the pilgrim and Chaucer the poet? How are they different? Why would Chaucer create a fictionalized narrator?

2. In what way does the "frame" of *The Canterbury Tales* become a tale?

3. Which tale should win the contest proposed by the Host? State your reasons why.

4. Select three tales and explore the relationship between the tale and the pilgrim who relates it.

5. What is the function of the "links" in *The Canterbury Tales?*

6. Compare two different ways in which Chaucer refers to the tradition of courtly love.

7. Discuss Chaucer's presentation of the clergy in three tales.

8. Trace the development of irony in one of Chaucer's tales.

9. Discuss Chaucer's use of the fabliau. Why are his fabliaux his most popular works today?

Bibliography

Ackerman, Robert W. *Backgrounds to Medieval English Literature*. New York: Random House, 1966.

Baldwin, Ralph. *The Unity of the Canterbury Tales*. Copenhagen: Rosenkilde and Bagger, 1955.

Baum, Paul F. *Chaucer's Verse*. Durham, N.C.: Duke University Press, 1961.

Bowden, Muriel. *A Commentary on the General Prologue to The Canterbury Tales*. New York: Macmillan Co., 1948.

Bronson, Bertrand. *In Search of Chaucer*. Toronto: University of Toronto Press, 1960.

Bryan, W. F. and Germaine Dempster, eds. *Sources and Analogues of Chaucer's Canterbury Tales*. Chicago: University of Chicago Press, 1941.

Chute, Marchette. *Geoffrey Chaucer of England*. New York: Dutton, 1946.

Clemen, Wolfgang. *Chaucer's Early Poetry*. London: Methuen, 1963.

Coghill, Nevill. *The Canterbury Tales*. Baltimore: Penguin Books, 1952.

Coghill, Nevill. *The Poet Chaucer*. Oxford: Oxford University Press, 1949.

Coulton, G. G. *Chaucer and his England*. London: Methuen, 1963.

Curry, Walter. *Chaucer and the Medieval Sciences*. New York: Oxford University Press, 1926.

Curtius, Ernst. *European Literature and the Latin Middle Ages*. New York: Pantheon, 1953.

Donaldson, E. Talbot. *Speaking of Chaucer*. New York: W.W. Norton, 1970.

Everett, Dorothy. *Essays on Middle English Literature*. Oxford: Clarendon Press, 1955.

French, Robert. *A Chaucer Handbook*. New York: Appleton-Century-Crofts, 1947.

Hitchins, H. L. *The Canterbury Tales*. London: John Murray, 1947.

Howard, Donald. *The Idea of the Canterbury Tales*. Berkeley: University of California Press, 1976.

Jordan, Robert. *Chaucer and the Shape of Creation*. Cambridge: Harvard University Press, 1967.

Kittredge, George. *Chaucer and his Poetry*. Cambridge: Harvard University Press, 1915.

Kluge, Friedrich. *The Language and Meter of Chaucer*. New York: Macmillan Co., 1915.

Kokeritz, Helge. *A Guide to Chaucer's Pronunciation*. New Haven: Whitlock, 1954.

Lewis, C. S. *The Allegory of Love*. London: Oxford University Press, 1936.

Lewis, C. S. *The Discarded Image*. Cambridge: Cambridge University Press, 1964.

Lloyd, J. L. *A Chaucer Selection*. London: George C. Harrop, 1952.

Lowes, John Livingston. *Geoffrey Chaucer and the Development of his Genius*. Boston: Houghton-Mifflin, 1934.

Lumiansky, M. R. *The Canterbury Tales*. London: John Murray, 1948.

Lumiansky, M. R. *Of Sondry Folk: The Dramatic Principle in The Canterbury Tales*. Austin: University of Texas Press, 1955.

McKisack, May. *The Fourteenth Century*. Oxford: Clarendon Press, 1959.

Malone, Kemp. *Chapters on Chaucer*. Baltimore: John Hopkins University Press, 1951.

Manly, J. M. *Canterbury Tales*. New York: Holt, 1930.

Mann, Jill. *Chaucer and Medieval Estates Literature*. London: Cambridge University Press, 1973.

Owen, Charles A. *Discussions of The Canterbury Tales*. Boston: D. C. Heath, 1961.

Pantin, W. A. *The English Church in the Fourteenth Century*. Cambridge: Cambridge University Press, 1955.

Robertson, D. W. Jr. *A Preface to Chaucer: Studies in Medieval Perspectives*. Princeton: Princeton University Press, 1963.

Robinson, Ian. *Chaucer's Prosody*. London: Cambridge University Press, 1971.

Robinson, Ian. *Chaucer and the English Tradition*. London: Cambridge University Press, 1972.

Rowland, Beryl, ed. *A Companion to Chaucer Studies*. Toronto: Oxford University Press, 1968.

Ruggiers, Paul. *The Art of the Canterbury Tales*. Madison: University of Wisconsin Press, 1973.

Southworth, James G. *Verses of Cadence: An Introduction to the Prosody of Chaucer*. Oxford: Blackwell, 1954.

Speirs, John. *Chaucer the Maker*. London: Faber, 1951.

Spurgeon, Caroline. *Five Hundred Years of Chaucer Criticism and Allusion*. New York: Russell, 1961.

Ten Brink, Bernard. *The Language and Meter of Chaucer*. London: Macmillan Co., 1921.

Wagenknecht, Edward, ed. *Chaucer: Modern Essays in Criticism*. New York: Oxford University Press, 1959.

Whittock, Trevor. *A Reading of the Canterbury Tales*. London: Cambridge University Press, 1968.